DEBT

AND THEY WHO CONTROL THE CREDIT OF THE NATION HOLD IN THE HOLLOW OF THEIR HANDS THE DESTINY OF THE PEOPLE

CONSPIRACY
OF
CREDIT

COREY P. SMITH

Published by The Credo Company — Memphis, TN

Copyright © 2013 by The Credo Company, LLC

All rights reserved.

Editor: Chandra Sparks Taylor

www.chandrasparkstaylor.com

Cover design: Felix Walker

Book design: Essex Graphix

www.essexgraphix.com

Library of Congress Catalog Card Number: On File

Library of Congress Control Number: On File

ISBN: 978-0-615-80956-4

Printed in the United States of America.

The Credo Company

4466 Elvis Presley Blvd., Ste. 260

Memphis, TN 38116

Conspiracyofcredit.com

www.credocompany.com

DEBT

AND THEY WHO
CONTROL THE CREDIT
OF THE NATION HOLD
IN THE HOLLOW
OF THEIR
HANDS THE DESTINY
OF THE PEOPLE

CONSPIRACY
OF
CREDIT

BY: COREY P. SMITH

DISCLAIMER

This publication is designed to provide accurate and authoritative information with regard to the subject matter covered. While all of the stories described in the book are based on true experiences, most of the names are pseudonyms, and some situations have been changed slightly for educational purposes and to protect each individual's privacy. It is sold with the understanding that the publisher is not engaged in rendering legal or other professional advice. If legal advice or other expert assistance is required, the services of a competent professional person should be sought.

CONSPIRACY OF CREDIT

■

"All Greatness of character is dependent on individuality. The man who has no other existence than that, which he partakes in common with all around him, will never have any other than an existence of mediocrity."

— James Fenimore Cooper

Author's Statement

There are many events that take place in our lives that are often unexplainable, but believe it or not the explanations are sometimes right in our faces. The word conspiracy is defined as the combination for a secret purpose. I have a completely different understanding of the word conspiracy, because of the circumstances surrounding my involvement with exposing the credit bureaus and those industries associated with them. Conspiracies are very real, but they are called conspiracies because you must be lead to believe the logical explanation presented by those who create the conspiracy. Remember, a sheep is considered the dumbest animal on the face of the earth, because it can be easily lead. I once read, "The human race is a herd. A herd because we concede to the herd mentality controlled and directed by a tiny few. This is how we are controlled. We have stopped thinking for ourselves and given our minds power away. Therefore, we follow the one in front in robotic fashion. And we are consumed by fear. Once our fear responses are activated, we rush to conform, even if we are aware enough to realize that what we are being asked to think, do and say is nonsense."

Consider how this is related to the euphemisms associated with religious institutional labeling the congregation as sheep or flock.

The political, religious, legal and credit institutions all interlock or work together in some way, to turn you into a two legged sheep. Most human beings walk around twenty three hours of the day as if they were counting sheep. This is hilarious to me because counting sheep is a mental exercise used as a means of lulling oneself to sleep. Consider the fact that we are taught at an early age to follow traditional ways of living our life to ensure success, such as going to school and making good grades, attending church and paying our tithes, voting for the right political candidate, whom will fight for our best interest, in regards to our living standards. Most of all paying our bills on time to ensure a good credit rating that we will never understand, but all of these are practices that come with a price that leads down a road to a mediocre life. These practices can all be associated with the idea of counting sheep. You see, these everyday routines are meant to induce boredom, while occupying the mind with something simple, repetitive, and rhythmic, all which are known to help humans sleep. Whatever your credit score is "Who cares!" A great credit score simply means you have successfully borrowed and repaid a lot of money. Which means you are good at managing debt and we are taught to achieve this goal. Your credit score says absolutely nothing about your financial security or your success in life. It is simply a metric system for lenders that focuses mainly on your payment history and what you owe others. Your real focus when it comes to credit is how can you remove yourself from its system. We are headed towards a micro chipped world and its taking place right before our very eyes.

■

"God gives you a certain talent.
It's whatever you can use to
inspire people the most."

— Will Smith

Introduction

This was a very difficult book for me to write simply because most people do not believe in conspiracies or they don't believe that our government would ever conspire with corporate gangsters seeking to enslave the masses of people who make this world work. Our government is like a husband who cheats on his wife and has a double life, and once the other life is revealed to us, we are in a state of disbelief. Most people do not understand the power of numbers. Numbers are used in the form of mathematics to predict things of the future as well as hide things from those who do not understand the laws of the universe.

Consider this statement made by Steve Perry, executive vice president of Visa Europe. He states, "cash is expensive, a cost on society and should be replaced by a cashless society." He goes on to say, "Why do you think supermarkets introduced cash back? It's because they want cash out of the system so there is less to manage. Processing a transaction on a card can be cheaper than handling cash." Now in order for anyone to understand the power of that statement, you must understand that the word VISA means to mark, or approve. I will explain in a later chapter what all of this means as it relates to a cashless society and credit.

■

"If a nation expects to be ignorant and free, it expects something that cannot be."

— Thomas Jefferson

THE HISTORY OF CREDIT BUREAUS

The only way to defeat any enemy is to know where he is as well as who he is and the weapons he has at his disposal. I'm going to give you a brief history of the three credit bureaus and the people who control them. There is no better way to gain social control over a population than information. This can be used as a defense or an offense. It can be used to create hope as well as fear and keep in mind, that HOPE is always greater than FEAR.

Let us first examine Experian, which is not even an American company. Experian's history dates back to 1897 when James Chilton helped a Dallas company record its customers' credit information in notebooks. The Chilton Corporation was a credit reporting agency that was acquired by TRW Information Systems and Services in 1989. TRW dates back to 1958 when Thompson Machine Products purchased Ramo Woolridge, an aerospace company headquartered in Los Angeles. Ramo Woolridge changed its name to TRW and was involved in many defense contracts. It was a major part of the military industrial complex.

In 1996, TRW sold its information systems and services to Tom Lee and Bain Capital Inc. for $1.1 billion. That same year Tom Lee renamed the company to Experian and sold it to Great Universal Stores (GUS) for $1.7 billion. Great Universal Stores is a one-hundred-year-old British holding company located in the United Kingdom. It also owns CCN Group, Europe's largest credit reporting agency. The same year that GUS purchased TRW from

Tom Lee, TRW and CCN Group merged to form what is now known as Experian. Experian's United States headquarters is in Costa Mesa, California. Its primary business is managing huge computer databases that store information on customer buying patterns and their credit history. Experian is paid each time a request is made for credit from a consumer. If there are more than two hundred million credit files stored in their database, how much do you think they are making a day from inquiries alone? Here is something else to think about: Experian is the fifteenth largest internet company in the world and owns LowerMyBills.com, the Home Shopping Network, Burberry, and Auto Check, which gives title reports on automobiles that are being sold or accepted for trade. This system is used by more than 97% of auto dealers in the United States. Later I will explain why this is important when it comes to guarding your personal information.

TransUnion had a very interesting beginning, that dates back into the 1800s and John D. Rockefeller who owned Standard Oil. Standard controlled oil shipping because of its monopoly on all the tank cars in the United States. It was doing great until the government stepped in to regulate its hold on the railcar industry.

After the government started creating problems for Standard Oil, it created the Union Tank Line Company a stand-alone corporation, in 1891. In 1911 the United States Supreme Court dissolved Standard Oil, making Union Tank Line an independent corporation. In 1919 Union Tank Line amended its name to Union Tank Car Company and begin to be publicly traded on the New York Stock Exchange.

Due to the nature of its business of leasing and selling oil tank cars and the possibility of profit loss, the company had to keep records on its customers.

Union Tank Car Company wanted its recordkeeping to be detailed, so they bought the Credit Bureau of Cook County in 1967. In 1968, Union Tank Car Company created TransUnion as its parent holding company. In 1972, it started a system that stored data on tapes and discs. In 1981, Union Tank Car Company sold TransUnion to the Marmon Group, a company that is privately owned by the Pritzkers of Chicago, Illinois during a time when the business was failing. The Marmon Group takes its name from the Marmon motor car that created the roadster that won the Indy 500 in 1911.

The Marmon Group was started in 1902 by Nicholas Pritzker. Today, the Pritzkers not only own TransUnion, they also own the Hyatt Hotel chain; Ticketmaster; Royal Caribbean Cruises; Accutronics; Hammond Organ Company; Pritzker Family Children's Zoo in Chicago; First Health Group; Nabisco: Elgin Grand Victoria Casino; Colson Corp; Pritzker Realty Group; and Pritzker Military Library. In 2004, the Pritzker family was number forty-seven on the list of the world's richest people. Most people are familiar with Equifax simply because of good marketing and advertising. Equifax is the leader when it comes to credit reporting agencies. It was founded by Cator and Guy Woolford, two brothers from Chattanooga, Tennessee. Cator was part owner in a local grocery store and kept credit history on their customers. Mainly for the town's Retail Grocers' Association.

5

In 1899, Cator talked his younger brother, Guy, into moving to Atlanta, Georgia, to start a business. Guy was an attorney, and at the time, his practice was not doing so well. Cator wanted to relocate to Atlanta because he saw opportunity there because of the population. That same year they started a business called Retail Credit Company. In the beginning, they sold a merchants guide, which contained the credit records of many citizens who lived in the city. The first guide was sold to a department store called J.M. High Company. In 1901, Retail Credit Company discovered that more money could be made in the life insurance industry, since in 1901 insurance was associated with credit, much like it is today. Retail Credit Company was incorporated in 1913, and by 1916, it was also involved in the mortgage business. During this time, there were major dollars being made in the insurance and mortgage businesses, and Retail Credit Company capitalized on those industries. Now can you see the same blueprint used today being created over fifty years ago. In 1970, Congress passed the Fair Credit Reporting Act, setting limits on the data that credit bureaus could have on one person. That same year Retail Credit Company's credit files became automated.

In 1971, Retail Credit Company began trading on the New York Stock Exchange. During this time, it was discovered that Retail Credit Company had many errors contained within its recordkeeping. As a result, it changed its name to Equifax, but still has many errors contained within its automated record keeping. Over the years Equifax has grown into a billion-dollar industry. In 1994, Equifax entered into a joint venture with Asociacion Nacional de Entidades de Financiacion to operate a Spanish credit reporting company. Equifax is a beast that has control of many insurance and healthcare entities.

This should be a warning to you as a consumer because it may be invading your privacy even when you are unaware. For years, Equifax and AT&T have been working on a sophisticated network allowing medical records to be accessed and downloaded by any doctor or specialist a person visits. Back in March 1995, Equifax and AT&T issued a press release stating they were joining to form its new Healthcare Information Services Group, a cluster of six businesses with more than fifty interrelated products and services. I don't know whether this ever happened or not. If it did, they control the nation's largest network repository of medical records. The reason I say if it did, is because they hide so much in plain site, but under different corporate umbrellas.

Keep in mind that Equifax owns HealthChex Inc., Osborn Laboratories, and Electronic Tabulating Services. Equifax and Lotus Development Corp are trying to put the names, addresses, and profiles of more than a hundred million consumers on a single CD-ROM. This system will enable a marketer to print up a mailing list of possibly every woman aged twenty-five to forty-five with a household income of more than $60,000 within a ten-mile radius. This sounds like the Accruint report provided by Lexis Nexis.

Remember TransUnion owns First Health Group, which is located in Downers Grove Illinois. The point I am trying to make is that this truly may be the mark of the beast and I don't want to sound cliché' with that statement.

Equifax has been in the insurance business since 1901, and even today one of its biggest clients is FedEx, which contracts out its property damage data to a division of Equifax called Insurance Information Services. Not only does Equifax handle commercial clients, it runs huge databanks for the auto and home insurance industry. This databank is called CLUE, short for Comprehensive Loss Underwriting Exchange. This system tracks your auto accidents and claims on your homeowners insurance. Equifax also controls Choice Point, which is on the New York Stock Exchange. Choice Point's database holds at least twenty billion social security numbers, credit and medical histories, motor vehicle registrations, job applications, lawsuits, criminal files, and professional licenses.

Choice Point owns a DNA analysis lab and facilitates drug testing for employers, another way to gather sensitive information since when you take a drug test you must show your identification. If after reading this brief history on the credit bureaus, you cannot see the puzzle being formed, I suggest you do your own research. Remember that you should try and invest in any company that makes money off of YOU!

If you would like to invest in Equifax, contact:

Equifax

Christy Cooper

Investor Relations and Shareholder

404-885-8300

■

"The world is governed by far different
personages than what is imagined
by those not behind the scenes."

— Benjamin Disraeli

Creation of Credit

It is August 6, 2001, and I wake up from a bad dream at 2:00am in the morning. As I awaken there was an unexplainable fear inside of me that I could not explain. The first thought to enter my mind was, I have a college degree, but yet I am sleeping in an apartment on the floor with no lights, not to mention the apartment was in someone else's name because my credit was to bad to even qualify for the apartment in my own name. It was at that moment I had an epiphany. I began to vent to myself mentally and I said to myself, "its credit!" That has to be the beginning of me getting out of this situation, and I'm going to be the first person to truly figure out the credit bureaus. At the time I was a substitute teacher at a local high school in Memphis, Tennessee, but the next week I would quit in order to pursue my quest to figure out the credit bureaus. There were many problems and questions to follow this decision that I was making. How would I survive with no money and no job?

In the mist of me trying to figure out the credit bureaus, I did realize one thing and that was my situation was not by coincidence and like so many others who were in the same boat, the first question that I ask myself was, "where did it all begin?"

It began my first semester of college, after I was bombarded with credit card offers and tricked into taking out student loans. I would have to say this may be the starting point for many of us, simply because we do not understand the cost of credit and how valuable debt is to those who create it as a trap for the less fortunate. In order for me to help you understand the power of credit and how it is a conspiracy, I must first give you its origin and explain its destiny. I pondered for many months wondering how I can tell my story. How can I get people to understand that credit is ultimately a trap, if you don't understand how it is used as a tool by the rich? There is an introduction to an album by a rapper named GAME, in which Gill Scott Herron say, "a lot of people are advocating that the rich get richer and the poor gets poorer, you see ladies and gentlemen its all just a game and many of you don't understand what is going to happen to you, the quality of your living depends entirely upon your ability to play the game." The problem is 98% of the world's population is not even in the game because they don't know the rules. The game of politics, education, religion, law and most of all CREDIT! These are the institutions that control the assembly lines of our society. They are all interlocked in some shape form or fashion and controlled by less than 1% of the world's population.

I will try to explain how credit began in a way that all who read this book will understand. There have been many stories told about the creation of credit dating back 3000 years ago to Assyria, Babylon. It is said, that debts were settled by one-third cash and two-thirds bill of exchange. This was done because paper money had yet to be invented. Another story told, was that, the first advertisement offering credit was in 1730 by, Christopher Thornton or Christopher Thompson, but who knows how accurate this information may be. This offer for credit was based on a system much like the one used today by many rent to own stores, such as Rent-A-Center and

Aarons Rent. This type of system was known as tallymen. They were called "tallymen" because they kept a record or tally of what people had bought on a wooden stick. One side of the stick was marked with notches to represent the amount of debt and the other side was a record of payments. There was also a guy by the name of Isaac Singer who was recognized with inventing consumer credit because he was trying to sell his sewing machines to potential buyers through installment plans. By the early 20th century there was another system introduced known as the shopper's plate. This was a buy now, pay later system.

In 1914, Western Union was one of the first companies to create a metal card, then known as Metal Money. This metal money was offered to their most prestigious customers, who were able to defer payments without incurring interest. By 1924, General Petroleum Corporation would soon follow suite with its own metal card that allowed employees to purchase gas and automobile related services. They would go on to offer the card to the general public. Ten years later, AT&T introduced the Bell System credit card, which opened the door for other service providers to offer their own credit cards. Remember in the last chapter I told you that Equifax and AT&T supposedly joined to form Healthcare Information Services Group in 1995. In 1950, Frank McNamara set up the Diner's Club Card. This was probably the first card that could be used at many different stores and businesses. The card was mainly created for businessmen to use for travel and entertainment. The unique thing about the Diner's Club card was that it gave its cardholders up to 60 days to make payment in full. Remember, the word credit comes from Latin, meaning "trust." But how can you trust a system that is designed to trick you into DEBT. Let me explain what I mean by tricking you into debt. The reason the Diner's Club card was probably the most significant in the evolution of credit was because it could be used for entertainment purposes. Remember, "To muse is to think, and to amuse is to entertain." Once merchants figured out that people spent more on entertainment when they used their Diner's Club card, they begin to find new ways to entice people into obtaining credit. What better way to do this, than allowing cardholders at least 60 days to make payment in full. This work for many merchants because most people who have credit tend to spend more, because the illusion of time is hidden in a billing cycle where debt increases as time passes. What I mean is that most people think time is an advantage in regards to them paying for purchases over a long period of time, but they forget the price is still accumulating interest. The first bank to try and capitalize on this charge-it concept was Franklin National Bank in New York. In 1951, they issued credit cards to customers who passed their screening process. The card could be used by customers at local businesses.

This system was similar to how credit cards work today. When a cardholder made a purchase the retailer verified authorization with the bank. Once the transaction was verified, the sale was approved. The bank would then pay the retailer and collect their money from the cardholder over time at a later date. In 1958, American Express introduced its card coupled with its famous slogan, "Don't leave home without it." But, the first revolving credit card was issued in the state of California by Bank of America. This BankAmericard was being advertised throughout the entire state, but what made it special was its cardholders had payment options. They could pay the debt in full or they could make monthly payments while the banks charged interest on the remaining balances. Bank of America saw this as an opportunity to make more money. They began issuing licensing agreements to different banks throughout the United States. This also gave them control as well. The licensing agreements allowed the other banks to issue BankAmericards and to interchange transactions through issuing banks.

However, this would eventually become a problem because charge card issuing and processing became too much for the banking industry to handle. Therefore, by 1966 fourteen US banks formed interlink an association with the ability to exchange information on credit card transactions. In 1967 four California banks formed the Western States Bancard Association and introduced the Master Charge in order to compete with the BankAmericard program. These two entities would eventually become what are known today as VISA and MasterCard. In 1977, BankAmericard became VISA and by 1979 Master Charge became MasterCard. This would indeed be the beginning of the End of Cash as we know it!

After I published my first book "How to OutSmart the Credit Bureaus," in 2005, I would soon find out the definition of paper terrorist. Most of all I would find out that the FBI and Postal Inspector would deem me a paper terrorist. I was attending Christian

Brothers University working on my Master's degree in Education, when one day I was checking my email and there was a message from the United States Postal Inspector. The message read, "You are the target of a federal investigation; please contact Inspector David T. Jones to discuss this matter. Immediately this email made me nervous, but at the time I didn't know it was about the book, or about me fixing people's credit. To put it plain and simple I ignored this email thinking it would go away, if I didn't talk to them. Needless to say that was not the case. Two weeks later, I would go to check my PO Box and there was a card stuck in the mailbox. It was from the postal inspector and it had the same message written on the back of the card. At this point I realized my desire to publish a book entitled "How to OutSmart the Credit Bureaus," had placed me under the radar. You know that radar that begins with all types of alphabets. Later that day I contacted my attorney and explained to him what was going on and asked him to contact the postal inspector on my behalf.

The crazy thing about it, he didn't consider it to be too serious and informed me that he would give the postal inspector a call. My nervousness and concern with being taken away from my family began to make me wonder, why did my book and the information that I provided in the book was so important that it would cause the FBI and Postal Inspector to want to question me. Well, I thought about how we have no say in whether or not our information can or should be included in the credit bureaus database.

Besides, most of us cannot afford not to be in their database, because we are not wealthy and at some point, you will need to borrow money for something, whether it is clothes, transportation, food, or most of all shelter. Therefore, credit is a big part of our life not to mention our survival in this credit driven society. Think about this, the credit bureaus get your personal information from banks and other financial institutions for free. All the credit history banks, credit card companies, collection agencies and insurance companies have in their databases is given to Equifax, Experian and TransUnion at no cost. The credit bureaus take that same information and sell it right back to the same lenders and companies they got it from. What is even funnier is that these same companies will market their credit products to you for a fee. Now, that is prostitution and pimping at its finest. It goes back to that statement, "the quality of your living depends entirely upon your ability to play the game."

You see the fact that I was providing some of the rules to the game, to those who are not supposed to know made me a threat or should I say a CREDIT TERRORIST. The majority of people do not understand that we are not customers, but in fact like cattle or sheep used as commerce for those corporations ran by the rich to create more wealth for themselves. Think about it, if you are not happy with the service you are receiving from any of the three major credit bureaus, you cannot take your business anywhere else. That's because you are not the customer, you are the business in which millions of dollars are generated everyday. Unlike all other business relationships that can terminate their relationships with other companies they are unhappy with, you cannot. What I mean by this is that creditors such as banks, department stores, mortgage companies, and retail chains have the ability to switch between credit bureaus, if they choose. All of this made me realize just how powerful the credit bureaus are and how much influence they have over politicians and lawmakers. Therefore, labeling individuals like me paper terrorist, who seek to educate people on the tricks and rights they can use to turn their credit into power is just another way to protect their business.

About two months had passed and I was learning more about credit and its power, if it was used to guarantee business loans. Also during this time my reputation of cleaning credit had become widespread and not just in my city, but nationwide. A friend of mine had educated me on shelf corporations and how they could be used with personal credit. These are companies that are aged, meaning their incorporation date is usually two or more years old. It hit me one day that instead of charging some of the individuals who were coming to me for credit repair, I would simply make them into what I called credit investors. What that meant was, I would actually pay them a fee to use their credit. That is, after I had cleaned their credit. I would have them sign a joint venture agreement, power of attorney and credit investor contract for the purpose of obtaining credit cards, bank loans, automobiles and real estate transactions. I have provided examples for you to examine.

Credo Company,LLC.

Letter of Understanding

Date: Nov. 30, 2006

ATTN: Prospective Credit Investors

The terms as outlined below shall be defined as a letter of understanding between Credo Company LLC, Inc. and any party interested in serving as an investor for potential/pending real estate acquisitions or refinancing, guaranteeing loans, and backing business ventures with their credit.

Let this serve as a general description of the investor position and transaction terms, specific facts and figures will vary from transaction to transaction and will be agreed upon by all parties as they are presented and secured.

Investor shall present Credo Company LLC, with a mid FICO score of no less than 700 and must apply and meet certain other criteria; specific to obtaining the lender approval based on lender's financing guidelines and criteria. Not every individual with this minimum credit score will qualify, as this may, in some cases, depend on various other factors, including, but not limited to, rent or mortgage history, employment status/history, state of residence, etc.

If approved, investor will not be required to contribute any funds toward the transaction. All closing costs, down payments, appraisals or any other associated fees/cost will be paid by Credo Company, LLC, its affiliates, clients, and/or from the proceeds of the transaction at closing.

The Investor will likely guarantee a company of choice (from Credo Company, LLC). However, if financing is not obtainable in that structure and is required to be held in the name of the Investor, it will held in the name of the Investor for a period up to 18 months, at which time refinancing or sale of real/personal property shall occur, within a period not to exceed 60 days.

Compensation to the Investors varies from transaction to transaction and will be addressed more specifically as they are presented. Compensation to be paid at the close of each deal.

_____
Credo Company, LLC

Nov. 30, 2006
Date

_____
Prospective Investor Signature

Nov. 30, 2006
Date

BY SIGNING THIS LETTER OF UNDERSTANDING, I ACKNOWLEDGE I HAVE READ AND UNDERSTAND THE GENERAL TERMS AND CONDITIONS OF THIS POSITION AND WISH TO BE CONSIDERED FOR ANY CURRENT AND/OR FUTURE FINANCING ACQUISITIONS FOR WHICH I MAY QUALITY. I UNDERSTAND THIS WILL INVOLVE OBTAINING A CREDIT REPORT AND MAY REQUIRE PROVIDING FURTHER PERSONAL AND/OR FINANCIAL DOCUMENTATION ON MY BEHALF, OF WHICH I AGREE TO PROVIDE AS REQUESTED.

19

Joint Venture Agreement

This Agreement made as of the __30th__ day of __November__, 2006 by and between Credo Company, LLC. C/o Corey P. Smith, (hereinafter referred to as "Credo Company LLC.") and __Michelle Alexeas__, (hereinafter referred to as "Investor") to form a joint venture.

THAT WHEREAS, Investor, pursuant to the Letter of Understanding dated __Nov. 30th 2006__ has a desire to invest in real estate, guaranteeing loans, business ventures, real property and personal property;

WHEREAS, Credo Company LLC is in the business of facilitating investments; and

WHEREAS, Investor desires Credo Company LLC to facilitate and administrate investments.

NOW THEREFORE, for and in consideration of the premises and the mutual covenants and conditions hereinafter set forth, the parties hereto agree as follows:

1. General Structure. Investor and Credo Company LLC., hereby form a joint venture of which they will purchase the property of __N.A.__ and/or obtain financing for __affiliate company__ Credo Company LLC will act as the Contract Administrator for the investment programs entered into by Investor and Credo Company LLC will check the daily operation, subject to terms hereof.

2. Purpose. The purpose of the Venture shall be to invest in __commercial lines of credit__

3. Term. This Agreement shall terminate at the consummation of the first and only investment program, however, no later than two (2) years after the date first written above unless otherwise agreed to by the parties. Notwithstanding any of the above, all monies continuing to accrue from the investment will be distributed to the Venturers according to the following:

   (1)   First, to pay (or to make provision for the payment of) all creditors of the Venture (including the parties hereto who are the creditors of the Venture) and the expenses of liquidation, in the order of priority provided by law or otherwise, in satisfaction of all debts, liabilities or obligations of the Company due such creditors and such expenses of liquidation;

   (2)   Second, to the establishment of any reserve which the parties hereto may deem reasonably necessary for any contingent or unforeseen liabilities or obligations of the Venture (such reserve may be paid over by the Parties to an escrow agent acceptable both Parties, to be held for disbursement in payment of any of the aforementioned liabilities and, at the expiration of such period as shall be deemed

advisable by the Parties, for distribution of the balance in the manner hereinafter provided in this Paragraph 2); and

(3)   Third, after the payment (or the provision for payment) of all debt, liabilities and obligations of the Venture in accordance with clauses (1) and (2) above, to the Parties or their legal representatives in proportion to balances in their respective positive Accounts as adjusted pursuant to Section 5 for all Venture operations up to and including such liquidation no later than the end of the fiscal year in which the Event of Termination occurs or, if later, within 90 days after the date of the liquidation of the Venture.

4. Capital Contributions. (a) The total amount of the capital to be contributed to the Venture shall be given by Credo Company LLC.

(b) Investor will provide use of authorized credit to be contributed to the Venture. The investor will not contribute any out of pocket funds to the Venture.

5. Net Profits. The Venture's distributable positive net profits will be paid 70% to Investor and 30% to Credo Company LLC.

a. The venture shall consist of one (1) eighteen month (18) month investment program in which Investor shall receive 70% of the profits per investments and Credo Company LLC, shall receive 30% of the profits per investment.

6. Indemnification. Each Venturer (an "Indemnitor") shall indemnify and hold harmless the other Venturer from and against any and all claims, demands, actions and rights of action which shall or may arise by virtue of anything done or permitted to be done by the Indemnitor (directly or through or by agents, employees or other representatives) outside the scope of, or in breach of the terms of, this Agreement. A Venturer who desires to make a claim against an Indemnitor under this Section shall notify the Indemnitor of the claim, demand, action or right of action which is the basis of such claim, and shall give the Indemnitor a reasonable opportunity to participate in the defense thereof. Failure to give such notice shall not affect the Indemnitor's obligations hereunder, except to the extent of any actual prejudice resulting therefrom.

7. Notices. Except as otherwise specifically provided herein, all notices hereunder shall be in writing and shall be given by registered or certified mail, return receipt requested (prepaid), at the respective addresses set forth below or such other addresses or addresses as may be designated by either party by written notice to the other.

Credo Company LLC
P.O. Box 11138
Memphis, TN 38118

Michelle Alexeas
4883 Haleuille Rd
Memphis, TN 38116

8. Entire Agreement. This Agreement supersedes any and all prior negotiations, understandings, and agreements between the parties hereto with respect to the subject matter hereof. Each of the parties acknowledges and agrees that neither party has made any representation or promises in connection with this Agreement nor the subject matter hereof not contained herein.

9. Modification, Waiver. Illegality. This Agreement may not be canceled, altered, modified, amended or waived, in whole or in part, in any way, except by an instrument in writing signed by all Parties. The waiver by either Party of any breach of this Agreement in any one or more instances, shall in no way be construed as a waiver of any subsequent breach (whether or not of a similar nature) of this Agreement by the non-breaching Party. If any part of this Agreement shall be held to be void, invalid or unenforceable, it shall not affect the validity of the balance of this Agreement. The Agreement shall be governed by and construed under the laws and judicial decisions of the state of Tennessee.

10. Assignment. Neither Party shall have the right to assign this Agreement or any of its rights hereunder to anyone without the written consent of the non-assigning Party. This Agreement shall inure to the benefit of and be binding upon each of the Parties hereto and their respective successors, assigns, heirs, executors, administrators and legal and personal representatives.

11. Attorney's Fees. In the event of any action, suit or proceeding by either Party against another Party under this Agreement, the prevailing Party shall be entitled to recover reasonable attorney's fees and cost of said action, suit or proceeding.

12. Independent Counsel. The Parties hereto understand and agree that each has had complete opportunity to have this Agreement reviewed and explained to him by independent counsel.

13. Governing Law. The laws of the State of Tennessee shall govern this agreement.

IN WITNESS WHEREOF, the parties hereto have executed this Agreement the day and year first above written.

AGREE AND ACCEPTED:

COREY P. SMITH   MICHELLE ALEXEAS

This was perfect for many of them, because most of my clients were low income people who had never even seen ten thousand dollars at one time. I felt like I had the perfect blueprint to amass lots of cash with very low risk in regards to affecting my client's credit. I was putting all of them behind Shelf Corporation, which meant the commercial loans would not be reported on their personal credit. Therefore no harm, no foul, even if a problem was encountered during the payback of the loan. All of this seemed like a mastermind plan, but sometimes things don't always go as planned. It was a Wednesday evening and I had just closed on a line of credit for fifty thousand dollars with Bank of America, when I got a phone call from my attorney stating, that I had been subpoenaed before a federal grand jury for possible bank and wire fraud.

■

"Whoever controls the volume of money
in any country is absolute master
of all commerce and industry."

— James A. Garfield

Credit Doublespeak

In George Orwell's novel *1984*, the concept of "doublespeak" was introduced. Simply put, "doublespeak" meant the deliberate altering of the meaning of words to the point where sometimes, words took on the exact OPPOSITE of their true meaning. What we hear in America all the time is "thank God I live in a free country," or "our soldiers fight to keep us free," and other statements of that nature. But what kind of a free country do we really live in, when to participate in the marketplace; we must put ourselves in economic prison. To make things worse some of us are taught to take pride in our poverty, and told not to forget where we came from. That is exactly what happens with credit reporting. This is where the "doublespeak" of fiction becomes the non-fiction version of 1984 that we are living. Rather than the government tracking people's every move, as it did in the novel, corporations now track our every move through credit reports and then they use our credit to deny us opportunities in the future using "doublespeak."

For example, most of us were probably taught that it is irresponsible to go into debt if you don't have to, but told you must have credit to get credit. And let us not forget the Debt Free sermons being preached all over the world. Yet, since the early 1980's, we have been told that to build good credit, we must go into debt. "Irresponsibility is RESPONSIBILITY" in this corporate dominated country of ours. You must get a credit card, or two credit cards or a loan to prove you are worthy of earning a good credit score. You must put yourself into debt, to show you are responsible, rather than simply being responsible by never going into debt in the first place. Most people are sold on the cliché, that there is such thing as good debt vs. bad debt. That absurd and twisted logic is our reality created by those who control credit.

For the last two hundred thirty years in this country, a person could go and get a job based on their resume, experience, references and an interview. According to the Society for Human resource Management (SHRM), 13% of employers check the credit of all job applicants.

But now, most companies and government agencies want the applicant to also have good credit. WHY? When an individual's personal financial situation was never of concern to an employer before, why has it become so now?

The answer is because the credit reporting agencies were not content with the fees they made simply by selling your private credit history to just lenders. The Credit Bureaus promote credit history as a measure of character and suitability for employment. There was more money to be made if these agencies could expand their clientele in any way. Remember the history of the credit bureaus. They peddled their services to employers, and in doing so are now not only making a fee every time you apply for a loan or credit card, but also each and every time anybody applies for a job. Of course corporations have to keep growing to please shareholders, so the for-profit credit reporting agencies didn't stop there. Credit bureaus went on to property management companies, so that every time you apply to rent an apartment somewhere, they get a cut through the housing application fees you paid, which are non-refundable. Because we are not even talking about credit anymore. We are talking about DEBT!

Once again, remember the history of the credit bureaus. They went on to make themselves necessary in the auto insurance world, as well. Ever wonder why you have a perfect driving record, yet your insurance premiums are higher than others with less impeccable driving history? It's because the credit bureaus have figured out a way to get insurance companies to pay for the credit reports they generate. Oh, and let's not forget Equifax owns CHOICEPOINT. When buyers of insurance were found to have an average credit score or low credit score, insurers decided that they could justify charging those customers a lot more money by categorizing them as "higher risk." So despite a good driving record, you are charged higher premiums anyway. There are forty nine states that now require every driver to have auto insurance, you have no choice but to get your credit checked and this makes the credit bureaus money and dings your credit score with an inquiry.

This trick enables auto insurers to make a lot more money off of good drivers and it allows the credit bureaus to make more money for themselves by opening up a new market where they can continue to cash in on the credit reports they generate. A win-win situation for the credit bureaus and the insurance companies. Where you live, where you work, how much you pay in interest and how much you pay in insurance premiums are no longer controlled by consumer preference or by the free market, but by giant corporations, who make billions of dollars off of you through the collection and sale of your private history, without any regard whatsoever as to how doing so may sabotage your future.

So now, to get a place to live, to get a job, to insure our cars or to get loans to start our businesses and buy our homes, we all need to pledge our allegiance to the credit bureaus, by taking out loans and credit cards in order to demonstrate that we are responsible with credit. All of this is a conspiracy to indoctrinate people into a lifestyle of indebtedness. What is even more insane is that unless we have applied for housing, or a job, or insurance or a loan, we cannot even obtain our credit reports without paying the credit bureaus ourselves. Oh! I forgot about your free annual credit report, but that's another story.

Think about this, your "scientific" FICO score can inexplicably be different at all four credit bureaus: Experian, Equifax, TransUnion and Novus/Innovus, you are then forced to monitor and pay for three different reports. The credit bureaus are not a service for YOU. Without your consent, they collect your personal information, from childhood, in order to sell it and make money off it. If you don't believe me, get a copy of your Lexis Nexis report. Forever In Credit Oppression (FICO) was designed as a tool to create a caste system. To add to this madness, many industries have cropped up now to make money off people's obsession with monitoring their credit reports. Let explain something. In the world of credit and banking, fraud is necessary and these industries expect fraud and allow a certain amount of fraud. What the public fails to realize is that it's like using propaganda in politics. You flood the media, newspapers, radio and internet to create a certain fear or emotional need to want something. It's like that old saying in the medical world, "there is more money in the treatment, than in the cure." Think about it, if fifty million people pay you ten dollars a month for a service that they could get for free, would you tell them? NO!

Credit card companies have "Zero Liability" insurance policies, which mean consumers are not held responsible for any fraudulent charges. Credit card protection is unnecessary because federal law limits your credit card fraud liability. A person could get a "FILE FREEZE" placed on their credit report and prevent identity theft. That is just one way, not to mention all the other tools provided by law enforcement agencies and the Federal Trade Commission.

There are people who paid for a service called "Life Lock." What a joke? The same guy who started "Life Lock" has filed thirteen identity theft reports since 2007. Which was clever, if you know how to use identity theft to your advantage. In 2008, Experian filed a lawsuit against Life Lock for placing bogus 90-day fraud alerts on over a 100,000 credit files maintained by Experian. Experian accused Life Lock of using false and misleading advertising to entice consumers into buying its credit protection and exploiting the system by acting as a middleman for a service that the credit bureaus are required to provide for free. Now how can he possibly come up with a way to protect your credit, if he can't protect his own? It seems that just about everyone has been duped by this marketed notion that "irresponsibility is responsibility." Consumers, under the fear of not being able to obtain more debt, blindly allow these credit bureaus to control them and to sell their identities, when in fact they can "OPT OUT," if they want. Its $10 per credit reporting agency, but it can be done. The FICO score has become a numeric status symbol that organizes people into castes. The high credit scores go to the rich and the lucky, while the low credit scores go to those who may have only made a mistake or two in their lives, those who suffered unexpected misfortunes, or those who started out life at an economic disadvantage and birth from an educational school system, that did not provide real lessons for economic success in life. The credit bureaus will try to persuade you that you can improve your credit in time, but that's a lie. It takes years to rebuild your credit and you can only do so by going into debt and then not having another misfortune, before you pay off that debt over an amount of time deemed acceptable by the credit bureaus. All the while, creditors are making interest off of your efforts to redeem yourself to an entity that frankly doesn't have any real authority. Hardworking Americans are victimized everyday by their credit reports. Perhaps they got behind on bills once; maybe they had an expensive medical emergency. Does that mean they should become homeless or jobless? America used to be a place where your car was your freedom and your home and job were automatic, if you were willing to work. How are we free when we are assigned a FICO score that predetermines our future opportunities? How can a single score possibly define a person? In this Land of Oz, that corporations have fashioned, Mr. FICO is the "man behind the curtain" who governs through a giant, intimidating mask and makes the final determination as to our place in American Society. Like Oz, Mr. FICO is made up and just like Dumbo the Elephant didn't really need his feathers to fly, you do not need credit to live a good life in America. You simply must learn the true logic behind credit and learn to play the game.

■

"Skillful use of words is vital in
getting the people to believe what isn't so."

— Unknown

Inquiries

I found myself becoming more intrigued with why inquires were so important when it came to credit. I mean really, should the credit bureaus penalize anyone for inquiries that they did not benefit from, especially the ones made by collection agencies or companies offering me pre-approved credit. One of the ways I would combat this tactic used by the credit bureaus was that I would send them a nice little letter accompanied with a police report. I would send the police report because it simply validated my claim of fraudulent inquiries placed on my credit as a result of identity theft. You see, when most people dispute inquiries, they often just tell the credit bureaus they did not authorize the inquiry. Well, the credit bureaus usually respond by stating that, "the inquiry is a statement of fact." What the hell is a "statement of fact?" NOTHING! Just a bogus excuse to keep the inquiry on your credit report in order to bring down your scores. You may be wondering why credit bureaus want you to have bad credit. Profit! Profit! Profit!

Let me explain how this works. The first way the credit bureaus make money is from selling the information they collect on consumers. Some of this information comes from credit card companies, student loan providers, collection agencies, banks, finance and utility companies. They also buy information from other credit bureaus. Most of the time they will contract with third party companies like Lexis Nexis, who often provide public record information or Call Credit who confirm application addresses and monitor significant events which may be indicators of credit risk. They are also global leaders in fraud detection software. The problem with this is credit bureaus must rely on the information they receive from these companies. This makes it difficult for them to prove the accuracy, timeliness and verifiability of the information given to them. This violates a major section of the Fair Credit Reporting Act. This section is 609 which requires proper verification according to established case law involving the credit bureaus having copies of the original signed credit application in their files. They are required to have a copy of the credit application that you signed when you opened the credit account with the creditor in their files. They are supposed to have it in their files to show that they verified the information before they placed it on your credit report. They must report 100% accurate information, report 100% verifiable information and report within the legal allowable reporting period, 7, 10, or 15 years.

Most of the time, we are the ones giving the credit bureaus information when we apply for credit. Once we get the credit, we continue to provide them with information based on how we pay our bills. Before all of the technology, most of the information collected about consumers was done manually by humans. Now it is all done by computers in automated fashion. This means whenever a creditors request a copy of your credit, the credit bureaus forwards the information electronically.

Additionally, regular updates from all "Subscribers" are required to be sent to all three credit bureaus monthly electronically using a system called "Metro 2." This system is totally computerized with no human interaction. The credit bureaus in turn sell the information collected on consumers in two formats. They are "Direct Marketing Data" and "Consumer Credit Report Data." Consumer credit report data is used by lenders to evaluate a consumer's credit risk and ability to pay back the debt. Lenders, landlords, employers, credit card companies, insurance companies, and licensing agencies buy consumer data from the credit bureaus. They pay a fee to obtain electronics copies of applicant's credit history. Now think about how many times that you have allowed someone to pull your credit report and multiply that by two hundred million. The credit bureaus are making a tremendous amount of money selling your information. Each time that you allow someone to pull your credit, the credit bureaus note this in your file.

The reason it hurts you so much is because of how the FICO scoring model is set up. The model considers frequent inquiries as an indication that you could be a big risk, not to mention if you actually were approved for the credit. So a word of advice would be not to apply for too much credit at one time. Many people will do this around the holidays, but in the eyes of lenders, you look desperate.

The credit bureaus also sell your information to marketing companies that want to reach consumers with a certain demographic, with the intention of selling you their products and services. For example, a local Toyota dealership wants to use direct mail to reach consumers who would potentially qualify for their 0% financing program. They may need the information on consumers within a 50-mile range, with a credit score of 730 or above. The credit bureaus provide this information to the Toyota dealership. These "Marketing Inquiries" must also be reflected in a consumer's version of their credit report, but they are not visible to anyone but the consumer, therefore, they do not affect the credit score. I will advise anyone to "Opt-Out" their information being sold to marketers. This will help you in repairing your credit, but most importantly, your information is kept private, and cannot be sold. If you want to opt out, go to www.optoutprescreen.com.

This will stop the credit bureaus from selling your information and making a profit off your personal information. Not all the data credit bureaus sell cost the same to creditors seeking to buy. Some information is more valuable than others, which allows the credit bureaus to charge more for that data. For example, as the consumers in the profile describe in the Toyota scenario may have high credit scores, they will qualify for the 0% financing. The dealership will sell a car, but not make any money on the financing. Since the dealer's priority is to move the old models off the lot quickly, they seek consumers with good credit. But consider this example. A credit card company, who charges outrageous fees and inflated interest rates to high risk consumers, wants to market to people with bad credit. The methodology behind this is consumers will be willing to pay more to have a credit card because they have bad credit. People with subprime credit are the people who make the banks the most amount of money in fees and interest. Now, which credit information can the credit bureaus charge the most money for? People with good credit or people with bad credit. So with that be said, why would the credit bureaus want you to have good credit? Since the companies who buy credit information about people with bad credit stand to make more money from that information. The credit bureaus charge them more money, than they would companies who buy information about people with good credit.

"The worse the score, the more money the credit bureaus make! Don't you think, it would follow that the credit bureaus have no incentive to correct inaccurate data. After all, the worse credit score, the more money the credit bureaus make on selling it. In addition to selling the bad data, the credit bureaus also make money on the dispute process.

I once read a study entitled "Automated Injustice," which had numerous cases compiled in a government study that exposed how the three credit bureaus make money off credit reporting errors. Think about this, the credit bureaus make the most money selling information about those people with the worst credit. These are same companies responsible for the dispute process and updating your credit file. That is like trusting the mouse not to eat the cheese. Since negative data is more valuable than accurate data, the credit bureaus have no real motivation to maintain accurate data in their system. All credit bureaus have a system they use to ensure that extending someone credit will not come back to haunt them. First, you must understand that much of the discrimination imposed against the poor and middle class is unseen to the general public.

I have provided you with examples pulled from an actual Experian and Lexis Nexis report. Pay attention to the information that I have outlined contained in each report. It will clearly show you how discrimination can be carried out.

Accurint

LexisNexis® Risk Solutions FL Inc.
Accurint Consumer Inquiry Department
P.O. Box 105610
Atlanta, GA 30348-5610

May 18, 2012

Corey P Smith
~~[redacted]~~
Memphis, TN ~~[redacted]~~

Reference #: ~~[redacted]~~

Dear Consumer:

We are sending this letter in response to the request you made for your Accurint Person Report. This

This is some of the information contained in your Accurint Report. I have provided a portion of that report.

Total Market Value - $64,700
Assessed Value - $16,175
Land Value - $4,700
Improvement Value - $60,000
Land Size - 7,500 Square Feet
Year Built - 1940
Data Source - A
Neighborhood Profile (2000 Census)
Average Age: 30
Median Household Income: $25,787
Median Owner Occupied Home Value: $45,500
Average Years of Education: 10
2395 PATE RD, MEMPHIS TN 38133-5109, SHELBY COUNTY (Oct 2011)
Name Associated with Address:
COREY P SMITH
Current Residents at Address:
DEWAYNE ARTRELL MILES
~~[redacted]~~60 MILES DEWAYNE
Property Ownership Information for this Address
Property:
Parcel Number -
Name Owner : MILES, DEWAYNE
Property Address: - 2395 PATE RD, MEMPHIS TN 38133-5109, SHELBY COUNTY
Owner Address: 2395 PATE RD, MEMPHIS TN 38133-5109, SHELBY COUNTY
Name of Seller : COOPER MARGARET L
Data Source - A
Neighborhood Profile (2000 Census)
Average Age: 29
Median Household Income: $60,250
Median Owner Occupied Home Value: $111,800
Average Years of Education: 13

These codes help the credit bureaus and creditors diagnose how well you will pay your bills, depending on which part of town you live. Through these geographic zip codes creditors or credit bureaus can distinguish whether you live in a low-income neighborhood, a middle-class, or a very affluent part of town. They will also be able to distinguish the statistics on how likely you are to become delinquent on your bills or file bankruptcy. This may sound like a conspiracy theory to some, but believe me when I tell you that their method is very real. The credit bureaus make money off your bad credit, not the good credit. They are in the business of selling your personal information to those companies who are willing to pay.

Under the Fair Credit Reporting Act (FCRA), you have the right to dispute incomplete or inaccurate information contained in your credit report. The credit bureaus must investigate all inaccurate information, unless your dispute is frivolous. The credit bureaus will use the word frivolous as a way not to honor your dispute because they claim more than 37% of the disputes they process are submitted by credit repair companies. They also claim that at least 30% of the total disputes filed are frivolous and abuse the system.

WOW!! What most people do not know there is an established process outlined by the FCRA. The problem is even though the law requires the credit reporting agencies to verify every account it reports on before reporting on it the fact is the lender never sends the credit application to the three credit bureaus. No lenders ever send the credit application therefore the credit bureau never verifies any of this information. Instead of sending the CRA a copy of the credit application to be verified, the creditor pulls the credit file of the consumer and the creditor verifies the information that the consumer puts on the credit application themselves. The verification process is done backwards. The law requires the credit reporting agency to verify the credit information not the creditor. This being the case, anything that is included in your credit bureau file can be removed if you request the credit reporting agencies right to report the item by forcing them to show you proof of verification that is supposed to be in their files. You can effectively remove both valid negative items as well as invalid items this way. While these rights may seem to benefit the consumer, once again we see that it only benefits the credit bureaus.

My father always taught me that life is a game of chess. It's about sacrifices, risks and rewards. Well, the very first time I went to meet the postal inspector and a detective from the Memphis police department, it was me moving a pawn. No matter how educated a person may think they are it's easy to make them form an opinion through site, therefore making them easy to fool. On that day, I wore a pair of Timberland boots, Roca wear jeans, and white tank top and about $60,000 worth of jewelry. My attorneys and I entered the room and I could sense the confused look they showed through their facial expressions. Now keep in mind, they never really knew who I was, only by name and old photos. They introduced themselves and then asked me to take a seat. After twenty seconds of silence, they asked my attorney to step outside in the hall. Once outside, I could hear the Postal Inspector tell my attorney, "that's not the guy, we want the mastermind." My pawn move worked, simply because these seasoned brains had made an assumption using their eyes. Well, needless to say, my attorney informed them that I was the guy. So they came back in the room and proceeded to ask me for a ten page handwriting sample and I obliged them in their request. One of the things I am gifted with is the ability to write in many different styles. Even good enough to fool a handwriting analyst.

After I finished the hand writing analysis, they took my fingerprints and a picture. That same day I flew to New York and once again I was on a quest for information, any information that would help me get money and I was sure I could find it in the Big Apple. The two-hour flight gave me some time to reflect on what happened earlier that day and why the feds would be so interested in someone who had a gift, when it came to credit. It reminded me of a book I read titled "Dumbing Us Down," by John Gatto. In his book there is a quote: "Do not destroy or kill your enemy, educate him for he is more valuable to you alive than dead." I found out what that meant after reflecting on my situation.

■

"Often the masses are plundered
and do not know it."

— Frederic Bastiat

Collection Accounts

It has been over five years since I had used my credit. Everything up until that point was acquired through the use of credit investors. I discovered several years prior, that I only needed to duplicate myself through other people. It wasn't that I was using them, but only using something they had no idea the power and monetary assets it could bring. Most people do not understand the weakness in which collection agencies operate under. First of all, they are second and third party creditors, meaning they are not the original creditor. You see when an account reaches 180 days past due, almost all lenders will charge the account off as a bad debt. Second, most of the time when they buy debt from the original creditor, they are usually only buying a "screen shot," or paper. I have provided an example of what a "screen shot," or "paper," looks like on the following page.

What this means is they purchase a portfolio of accounts and they have the option to purchase copies of all the documentation with the file. This documentation does not come free, and can triple or quadruple the price of the portfolio. Collection agencies almost never purchase full documentation, so they are unable to provide legitimate validation. Third, they are buying accounts as a form of investment. As, I am sitting at home one day looking over my credit report, I count over 36 negative accounts. To make things worse 24 of these accounts have been bought by collection agencies. In a way, I become very discouraged because it has been several years since I have tried to fix credit of this magnitude. But, I had to remind

DEBT VALIDATION

PRIOR/ORIGINAL CREDITOR: HSBC CONSUMER LENDING USA/ HOUSEHOLD FINANCE
90 CHRISTIANA ROAD
NEW CASTLE, DE 19720

ORIGINAL ACCOUNT NUMBER: 84520100387096   OPEN DATE: 04/15/2004

BALANCE: $20,894.17   LAST PAYMENT DATE: 08/30/2004

PRINCIPAL: $14,814.24   CHARGE-OFF DATE: 07/11/2005

INTEREST: $6,079.93   INTEREST RATE: 22.00 %

FEES: $0.00

PERSONAL INFORMATION

Name	MECHIA Q ████IGA█	Social Security #	XXX-XX-█06█
Address	25████RKS ST		
City/St	MEMPHIS TN		
Zip	██1068536		

Please make payment to:
Asset Acceptance LLC
PO Box 2036
Warren, MI 48090
Please include account number on your payment.

**THIS IS AN ATTEMPT TO COLLECT A DEBT AND ANY INFORMATION OBTAINED
WILL BE USED FOR THAT PURPOSE.**

myself that I am the best when it comes to fixing credit. I see all of these people on television like Kevin Trudea, Suzanne Orman, Dave Ramsey, and John Ulzenhemier, talking about credit and debt, but to me they are all a joke. I say that because they fail to give people real information they can use.

I am quickly reminded of my confidence of being the best. One of the first accounts I choose to dispute was an American General

Finance account that had been bought by Credit One also known as One Solutions. The first phone call I made to them I end up talking to a collections manager by the name of Robert Head. I inform him that this account is a result of identity theft and I am disputing it as such. I also told Robert, that I was going to be sending him a police report along with a notarized validation of debt request. Robert was infuriated and told me that police reports are a dime a dozen and if I sent him one he was going to put it in the shredder. He also informed me that he knew all the laws and tricks that people like me play when it comes to disputing collection accounts. I laughed at Robert and stated to him, that he had no idea who I was and that I would get the last laugh. A week later, I got a letter from Credit One refusing to honor my police report and an Affidavit for Destroyed Instrument (page ????).

This would make some people panic, but not me because I knew other ways of getting Credit One's attention. If a debt is charged off by the original creditor that means it has been removed from their balance sheet as uncollectible from the borrower. It must be validated according to the FDCPA, should it come back in some other type of collection by means of an agency working for the original creditor or a third party that purchased the account. The first thing I did was send Credit One and the original creditor, American General Finance, a Sworn Affidavit of Denial, and then I filed a complaint against Credit One with the Better Business Bureau and the Department of Consumer Affairs in my state. Notice actual documentation on the page ???.

AFFIDAVIT OF DESTROYED INSTRUMENT

STATE OF INDIANA
COUNTY OF VANDERBURGH
CITY OF EVANSVILLE

The undersigned being duly sworn, states and deposes as follows:

1. My name is Emily Blemker, I am over 18 years of age. I have never been convicted of a felony. I am capable of making this affidavit and am fully competent to testify to the matters stated herein. To the best of my knowledge, each of the matters stated herein is true and correct.

2. I am employed by American General Finance (AGF) as Agency & Sold Portfolio Coordinator.

3. As part of my duties, I am custodian of certain business records of AGF. I certify that as of April 8, 2005, Corey Smith, SS#■■■■1855 entered into an open line of credit and/or credit card loan agreement with AGF with the account number of 44921204. As of November 30, 2005 there was due and payable a sum of $3,844.92 owing.

4. The information contained herein was obtained through the files, records and computer screens of AGF and maintained in its regular course of business.

5. AGF has performed a due and diligent search of its records, and the original contracts in this matter have been lost, stolen, destroyed, or are no longer accessible to the deponent.

6. This affidavit is to be treated as the original document for all purposes and if any originals are discovered, they will be submitted to the court for cancellation.

x _Emily Blemker_
American General Finance, Inc. (AGF)

Emily Blemker
Printed name of Affiant

Sworn and subscribed before me, the ___ day of December, 2010.

MY COMMISSION EXPIRES _____

x _____
NOTARY PUBLIC

NINA D. FOLSOM
Resident of Vanderburgh County, IN
Commission Expires February 27, 2016

48

GENERAL AFFIDAVIT
State of Tennessee
County of Shelby

BEFORE ME, the undersigned Notary,
_____Jeffery Young_____, on this 14, February,
2011, personally appeared _____Corey P. Smith_____, known to
me to be a credible person and of lawful age, who being by me
first duly sworn, on his or her oath, deposes and says:

I deny that this is my debt and if it is my debt, I deny that it is
still a valid debt and if it is a valid debt, I deny the amount
requested is the correct amount. I acknowledge this debt was
established without my knowledge and I have no contractual
agreement with Credit One LLC, American General Finance
(AGF) or Emily Blemker.

_____Corey P. Smith_____
[signature of affiant]

Corey P. Smith

Memphis, TN 38███

Subscribed and sworn to before me, this _14_ day of February,
2011.

NOTARY SEAL:

_____
[signature of Notary]

_____Jeffery Young_____
[print name of Notary]

NOTARY PUBLIC

My commission expires:
___Apr 6_____, 20 _14_ .

49

CONSPIRACY OF CREDIT

WHAT DO I DO NEXT?

The Better Business Bureau has forwarded a message from the business to you and are waiting for your comments.

PICK YOUR NEXT STEP:

Accept Business Response →

Reject Business Response →

For more detail on these choices, **click here**.

Message received from the business about your complaint

Sent Via:	Email (ODR)
From:	BBB/Greater New Orleans Area
To:	Mr. Corey P Smith
To Email:	**Mr. Corey P Smith**
Subject:	Message received from the business about your complaint
Date Sent:	3/1/2011 1:36:55 PM
Attachments:	20110301-135735 business response.pdf

Click here for printer friendly version

BBB/Greater New Orleans Area
710 Baronne St., Ste. C
New Orleans, LA 70113
Phone: (504)581-6222 | Fax: (504)574-9110

03/01/2011

Corey Smith
~~————————~~
Memphis , TN 38___

Dear Corey Smith :

This message is in regard to your complaint submitted on 2/18/2011 12:00:00 AM against Credit Solutions L. L. C. Your complaint was assigned ID 8507361.

We have received a reply from the company, a copy of which is below or attached.

In order that our records may be complete, please indicate if the company's offer will satisfactorily resolve this complaint. Unless we hear from you within two weeks of the receipt of this letter, we will have to consider the matter settled.

Also beware that there are times that the debt is also used as a tax loss by a creditor. That means they cannot be collected at a later time as the collector would then obtain UNJUST ENRICHMENT. If, the debt cannot be verified and validated by the debt collector and the collector continues collection activity you may have grounds to sue under the FDCP.

Remember that you can take these same steps when you are faced with this problem. The reason why all these tactics I used were so critical was because there is a paper trail. You see collection agency have to honor a valid police report and most of all because collection agencies are a business; they seek funding and working capital from lenders as well. Therefore they do not want a bad rating with the Better Business Bureau or Department of Consumer Affairs. Remember, when I told you that collection agencies are buying debt as an investment. Well that is what that little thing called Unjust Enrichment means and can be used in the court of law, if you ever needed to take it that far. Unjust enrichment is when a collection agency buys a $10,000 debt for $200 dollars, then conspires to reap benefits by denying consumers validation of debt request in a scheme to artificially inflate the balance due by adding penalties and interest of up to 200 or 300 percent. Think about it. How can they be entitled to anything over the $200 dollars they spent? It was an investment to them and they rely on the consumer's ignorance, financial distress and lack of legal representation to secure a judgment. Debt collectors have learned it's not cost effective to provide proper validation of debt, it's easier to file suit because most people will not answer the suit. About three weeks later I am on the phone with another creditor and I get an incoming call from a strange number, it's Robert Head. He says, "Hello Corey, this is Robert how about we just remove the account from your credit and go away?" I am in a state of disbelief, simply because I expected Credit One to put up a better fight. But, like I said, "Last Laugh." The proof is shown below.

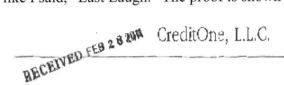

CreditOne, L.L.C.

Ruth Burton   February 24, 2011
Better Business Bureau
710 Banone Street, Suite C
New Orleans, LA 70113

Re: Our File # AG283978
       Corey P Smith
       Your File # 8507381

Dear Ruth Burton;

I am responding to a complaint submitted by Corey Smith concerning the above referenced account. We have contacted American General Finance and verified that the account was previously determined to be fraud. We have closed the account in our system and submitted deletion requests to the appropriate credit reporting agencies.

Sincerely,

William Rice
Collection Manager

THIS IS A COMMUNICATION FROM A DEBT COLLECTOR

You see, Robert knew the Fair Debt Collection Practices Act supports my right to demand a validation of debt, documentary proof that I owe exactly what is claimed. The Act places this right in such high regard that the collector is prohibited from taking any collection action until the validation is provided. If they do not, you can sue for a violation. Often the collector has no proof that you owe and knows it. Not only that, the Act requires that you be warned of your right to validation in writing within the initial communication from the collector. If they do not warn you in the first communication, the collector has five days to mail it to you. If they do not, you can sue.

The one thing that most people forget is that a collection agencies only objective is to get money from you, no matter how bad you are struggling in life. Think about this, why would you pay a debt that has already ruined your credit and you don't have the money to pay it. If you did, it wouldn't be on your credit. It equates to this, people in the church who have a utility bill that is due, they have the money to pay it, but instead put the money in church. Their rational for this is usually that God is going to bless them ten fold. Remember the Sheep? God has already blessed you with the money to pay your utility bill. Case in point: Paying off a collection account is not going to improve your credit, no matter what Suzanne Orman or Dave Ramsey tell you, IT WILL NOT! The poor credit history is still there. Bad credit is like a treadmill, if you try to always play by the rules, you will be running in place, but going nowhere. Once I discovered how effective this tactic was, I used it with each collection agency that chooses to give me a problem. Needless to say, it was effective each and every time. The goal of the creditors and collection agencies are to keep you in debt, but you must find ways to utilize debt to your advantage because it will always be there. I often smile when I watch television and I see all of these preachers talking about being debt free. Honestly, you can never be debt free, simply because there will always be payment for shelter, food, clothing, utilities, transportation and most of all you cannot function in our society without the use of credit. Therefore, you will never be debt free, so recognize this bandwagon mentality and don't get on it.

■

"Our monetary system would not work
if all of the world's bankers
were not in collusion."

— Merrill M.E. Jenkins

Mathematics of Credit

I remember taking a tour of a prison once and there were several things that I noticed. One was that many inmates who had mental issues were still being locked up although they were deemed mentally challenged. The tour was conducted by one of the Lieutenants in the prison and as we were touring, he stopped one of the inmates to prove a point. He stated, "Most people in our society like being told what to do and those inmates were a reflection of this idea. He picked a random inmate and told him to spread his legs and open his hands so that we may see the inside of his palms. Then all of a sudden, he told the inmate to clap his hands. The inmate did everything the Lieutenant asked him to do without questioning him as to why he was even stopped. The Lieutenant explained to us that most people in society react in the same manner they never question why certain things are asked of them, whether it is religious leaders, educators, politicians and most of all law enforcement. Fyodor Dostoyevsky once stated, "The degree of civilization in a society can be judged by entering its prisons."

One of the things that many people fail to realize is that credit is all based on numbers. That means your ability to maneuver in this life without having access to cash depends on your credit score. Credit scores are based on mathematical formulas. Most people associate their credit score with the word FICO, which means Fair Isaac Corporation. FICO is the company that pioneered credit scoring and those numbers range from 300 to 850. Their scoring model are created by statisticians who create algorithms that basically can predict the credit and spending habits of the average consumer. If you wanted to know the mathematical formulas used to calculate your credit scores it would be impossible. The mathematical models are trade secrets or proprietary intellectual property. The Fair Isaac Corporation does not publish its mathematical formulas anywhere. They use a method known as multivariate analysis that statisticians use to see how numerous inputs affect a single output. Their model basically made it easier to read credit reports because the algorithms reduced people to numbers, although the average consumer does not understand the complexity or meaning of their FICO score. To try and simplify their scoring model FICO once released a graph showing how certain mistakes could affect your credit. They also offered a service known as the Fair Isaac Corporation personalized FICO simulator. The simulator basically uses your actual credit history to run some what if scenarios.

For example, FICO revealed that a bankruptcy could drop your score up to 240 points, foreclosure up to 160 points, maxed out credit cards up to 10 points and someone who pays their bill 30 days late up to 80 points. The key word in all of this is mathematicians and predict. Do you think the average person can relate to Bozo the clown better, or Albert Einstein? You see most people are just pawns in a game of have and have not's.

If you think numbers don't mean anything, consider this, math played a major role in the creation of the internet, text messaging and search engines such as Google and Yahoo. Just like mathematicians created the FICO score, a guy by the name Hans Peter Luhn invented was known in the credit card industry as the Luhn formula. The Luhn formula is used to generate credit card numbers that uses a combination of digits that must be divisible by 10 once they are added up. Think about this, there are 16 digits on VISA, MASTERCARD, and Discover cards, 15 on American Express, and 14 on Diners Club/ Carte Blanche cards. On Visa and MasterCard's, the first six digits identify who issued the card and the next nine digits is the account number. Here's the catch. The last digit on your credit card is known as a "check number" or "key" that verifies if the card is legit.

So go ahead, pull your card out and add up all the numbers, then see if it's divisible by 10. You are probably asking yourself, what does all this have to do with credit? Algorithms! An algorithm is a mechanizing device that always gives you a logical and predictable conclusion. These algorithms are also used on human beings. Andrew Kahr proved this by basically making people believed they were apart of a special group. Kahr created zero percent teaser rates and two percent minimum monthly payments, to cash rebates by invitation only, which was a trick. I believe that Kahr understood people who poor and educated by a system of manipulation. The reason I say this is because he once stated, "Is any bit of food too small to grab when you're starving and when there is nothing else in sight?" Believe it or not this is how most think and it starts during the first years of our education. As John Gatto explained his book "Dumbing Us Down," that schools were designed by Horace Mann,

Sears and Harper of the University of Chicago and by Thorndyke of Columbia Teachers College to be instruments for the scientific management of a mass population. Schools are intended to produce, through the application of formulas, formulaic human beings, whose behavior can be predicted and controlled. So we are all being defrauded from the beginning of kindergarten. The Luhn check formula is basically used to detect FRAUD! There's that word again.

Remember a complex problem is always solved with a simple solution and identity theft is a complex problem, if you listen to the credit bureaus, who basically allow much of the fraud that takes place. One of the reasons, I was a great interest to the FBI was because I was using identity theft to my advantage. There are over eight million people a year, who are victims of identity theft and trying to distinction between the real victims and fake ones can be quite difficult. In the book "How to Outsmart the Credit Bureaus" there is a chapter that talks about creating a new credit file by changing your name ,using a tax id or cpn number. This is possible because of how the credit bureaus identifying procedures work. When I was in the process of cleaning my credit, I discovered that credit bureaus have a mix department. I was constantly disputing things on my credit report and I was always sending documentation into support my claim. One day I was on the phone with an Equifax employee inquiring about a letter sent back to me stating an account was removed, but maybe a month later that same account would reappear. She told me that, because my file was so long, I had more than one file and sometimes this would cause old or deleted information to be mixed with my updated credit file.

According to Chi Chi Wang, if an id theft only adopts your first name and social security number, but not your last name or address, the algorithm used by credit bureaus to "merge" information often will incorporate the thief's information into your credit file. This is the reason it was so easy for some people to create new credit files, just by changing their names or using a tax id number. Although the credit bureaus do have a mix department and sometimes information can reappear on your credit file, many people become victims of "re-aging." Re-aging is when collection agencies or debt buyers purposefully put negative accounts back on your credit file and change the first date of delinquency. This is a problem because the seven year period in which negative information can be reported on your credit start with the first date of delinquency. Most people think that it is the charge off date or date of last activity. Debt buying is a billion dollar industry and they are not in the business of fair and accurate credit reporting. This works well with the credit bureaus, because remember they too make money off your bad credit. I will talk more about collection agencies in Chapter 4. I will end this chapter by providing you with a brief description of how the credit bureaus database utilize a matching system to identify and create new credit files. The type A system that Equifax and Experian use allow consumers' identifying information to be entered into the computer system in an attempt to match existing data. If no matching information is found, a new file is created. The credit bureaus' computer systems are very sophisticated but simple. Their matching system is designed in the following format:

1. LAST NAME—The computer only identifies the first ten letters of the last name. Letters must match an existing file, or a new file will be created and the computer will stop the search. If a match is made, the computer will proceed.

2. FIRST NAME—If the last name matches an existing file, the computer will continue by searching for the first three letters of the first name. If the first name matches an existing file, the system will then proceed to match other identifying information.

3. MIDDLE INITIAL—After the first and last names have been matched, the computer will check for the middle initial. If it finds a match, it will continue.

4. SPOUSE—If a person is married, the spouse's first initial will appear after the file holder's middle initial. If the person is not married, the computer will try to match other identifying information.

5. NUMERIC ADDRESS—When all the above information matches, the computer will try to match the first five digits of the numeric address.

6. STREET NAME—The computer will match the numeric address with the first letter of the street.

7. ZIP CODE—The computer will match the address that is retrieved with zip code. If the consumer has been at the address more than three years, the computer will stop. A search showing other people with similar names and addresses will cause the computer to merge the files, and a flag will be added to it.

8. PREVIOUS ADDRESS—If the consumer has not lived at the residence longer than three years, the computer will check previous addresses. The credit bureaus' computer system can hold up to ten previous addresses, but will usually list only the last three.

9. DATE OF BIRTH—The system will match the consumer's year of birth only.

10. SOCIAL SECURITY NUMBER—The computer will match all the previous identifying information with the last four digits of the consumer's Social Security number. If the number does not match the previous reported number, a flag will be added to the consumer's credit file. The credit bureaus also maintain files on employer identification numbers (EIN) and taxpayer identification numbers (TIN).

If you are wondering if the following information is accurate, here is something to consider. When you call to request a copy of your credit report, take note of all the identifying information the automated computer system requests from you then think about the information that is required when you go to fill out a credit application. The credit bureaus need all of the other identifying factors such as your name, address, and date of birth because they are not authorized to use your full Social Security number for the purpose of establishing a credit file. Because you give them so much information when you fill out a credit application, it is easy for the computer system to use the previously described method.

If the credit bureaus were authorized to use your Social Security number to establish your credit file they would have access to more than the last four digits of your Social Security number when searching the pacer system for those individuals who have filed bankruptcy.

Your Social Security number was created during the Great Depression for the purpose of establishing basically a savings account for individuals to retain after retirement however, it has turned into something more than just a savings account number, and part of that is because that bank (Social Security) is broke.

■

"There is no surer, more subtle means
of overturning the existing basis of
society than to debauch the currency."

— John Maynard Keynes

E-OSCAR

The FBI are like ghost, I mean they are always around watching, listening, and waiting to put the fear of God in anyone they have placed under their radar. I love my family very much and so I make it a habit to do certain things such as take my kids to school every chance I get. This particular morning would be unforgettable, simply because the FBI would finally make their move to arrest me. It was a very cold morning in February of 2007 and almost two years had passed without any communication between me and the FEDS. I returned home from dropping my oldest daughter off to school, when I noticed several government vehicles parked in front of my home. To make things worse, they were taking pictures of all the luxury cars parked in front of my house. At first I drove pass my home because it became obvious to me they had no idea what type of car I was driving at the time. I had just purchased a black 2007 S550 Mercedes Benz from a dealership in Atlanta under the name of a shelf corporation I had set up in Georgia. With that being said, I simply drove right passed them and parked three streets over from my house.

I got out getting a closer look on foot. I got as close as I could to my house, so that I could see what they were doing. There was a home being built one street over from my house and so I watched from inside the vacant house. I noticed they had entered my home as well as called tow trucks to take the cars parked in my garage. As I stood there and watched, it dawned on me that all of this was about credit and my ability to manipulate a system that had been monopolizing and manipulating over 200 million Americans already. It made me think about something Alexander Solzhenitsyn once said, "When truth is discovered by someone else it loses something of its attractiveness." You see inaccuracies and errors is the key to the credit reporting system. The major credit bureaus Equifax, Experian, and TransUnion conduct their credit reporting systems through an automated system known as E-Oscar, which is a for profit entity.

Credit bureaus are private and public for-profit companies that collect data on the credit history of people, and then sell to the commercial and financial enterprises that extend credit. The bureaus get this information from many sources and consolidate it into one database that provides reports to different creditors to show all the credit history related to a particular person or company.

Before the bureaus can collect any credit information, they must enter into an agreement with the different institutions that hold this data. These institutions are normally known as members or affiliate credit institutions.

These companies make an agreement with the credit bureaus to give them information about the credit history of their customers in return for having access to the credit bureaus' database known as E-OSCAR. The terms of the agreement usually state what information will be provided, the number of times per month it will be given, and the responsibility of each company to guarantee successful data transmission. The agreement also includes confidentiality clauses, data security, and payment for service. When the credit information comes into the credit bureaus' databases from the different companies, they all are updated by way of a nine-track tape or ribbon. This is simply an electronic update each month from the different companies. When updating, businesses use a digit code: 1-on time, 2-thirty days late, etc.

The software system E-OSCAR performs a quality check on the information, such as looking for format errors and data that does not correspond to the codes I mentioned earlier. Credit bureaus do not verify the content of the information they receive. The company sending the credit information usually does this. E-OSCAR is the heart of the credit bureaus. If you can understand it and the laws that govern it, you can basically control your credit file.

I have provided you with parts of a letter that was written by Ms. Jennifer J. Johnson, former secretary for the Board of Governors of the Federal Reserve System, in which she speaks about the databases the bureaus use to maintain information.

"Generally, while the vast majority of disputes about information furnished to consumer reporting agencies are received directly from consumer reporting agencies rather than consumers, banks treat all disputes similarly, investigating promptly and within the Fair Credit Reporting Act timeframes. In many cases, the process of receiving disputes from consumer reporting agencies and responding is automated."

Later in the letter she states, "Banks rely on their own records to submit information in an automated fashion, using the codes, forms, and formats required by the consumer reporting agencies. The files (tapes) are then submitted to the consumer reporting agencies on a monthly basis and uploaded to their systems."

I put the last statement in bold because I wanted you to understand that almost every verification process that takes place between banks (credit card companies) is all done by codes and is automated. Remember earlier when I told you that creditors update their information on their customers by using what is called a ribbon? This is what Ms. Johnson is talking about in the sentence that I have in bold print.

Ms. Johnson goes on to talk about the E-OSCAR system: "That system uses dispute type codes to identify the nature of the dispute in order to guide the furnisher in its investigation. After investigating, furnishers respond with the appropriate automated code, either verifying that the information is correct or providing corrected information." Remember everything is verified by automated codes. This means limited information is provided, which makes it hard for the consumer.

She adds, "The E-OSCAR system has the advantage of expediting the dispute process so that furnishers and consumer reporting agencies can comply with the tight deadlines of Fair Credit Reporting Act. By nature, an automated system means less can be transmitted and considered. In some cases, the dispute codes lack sufficient specificity of the nature of the dispute, sometimes because the consumer has provided insufficient information. In those cases, the furnisher relies on its own internal data information and process to investigate."

Notice the words in bold. This very statement is usually what happens when you, the consumer, try to take the traditional route of questioning incorrect accounts on your credit report. I am sure almost every person who has tried to dispute inaccurate information on his or her credit report has received a letter from the credit bureau stating, "The account information has been verified as belonging to you." That is because the agencies are relying on their own internal system. This is why you must avoid disputing via the internet.

E-Oscar allows creditors to electronically communicate with the credit bureaus. E-Oscar gives the credit bureaus the ability to receive what is known as a BatchInterface. A batch interface is when there are large amounts of disputes submitted in electronic formats. These formats are transmitted using three digit codes. These electronically transmitted codes are known as Automated Consumer Dispute Verification forms (ACDV). There are about 26 of these dispute codes given by the E-Oscar system. They include disputes such as: paid as agreed, not mine, no knowledge of account. This basically creates a one sided playing field because the consumer cannot provide any additional documentation to defend their claim of inaccuracies. This means credit bureaus can accept whatever creditors choose to do when it comes to resolving a dispute or an investigation with consumers. The reason why credit bureaus pretty much "parrot" whatever the creditors decide is because consumer disputes cost money, and many of the employees are told to be fast without any real inquiry. It is a system designed for profit not accuracy. You can read more about this in the section on Outsourcing. Therefore, it's up to the creditor to make the decision in regards to what is accurate and what is not. Thus, if the creditor instructs the credit bureau to keep the information being reported, there is nothing the consumer can do to really change that decision. This alone is a violation of the Fair Credit Reporting Act because no matter how much supporting documentation the consumer can provide it doesn't mean anything because the E-Oscar system will only provide the creditor with a three digit code. The Fair Credit Reporting Act requires that the credit bureaus must use "all relevant information" provided by the consumer.

E-Oscar is a system that converts what is supposed to be detailed dispute letters into these two or three digit codes. This makes it easier for the credit bureaus and the creditors, but its bad news for consumers. The code is sent to the creditor who is reporting the information to the credit bureaus without any supporting documentation. That means any evidence that you have to support your dispute claim is obsolete. This is the very reason you should not do anything on line when it comes to the credit bureaus. All the gimmicks that you see on TV or internet about free reports and credit monitoring is all for profit and truly don't provide any real service. Do not be fooled by products like "Life Lock," you the consumer can put a freeze on your credit report through the credit bureaus for free. Just pay attention to how the credit bureaus are trying to drive you to do everything on line. You might think that it's fast and easy, but you are really putting yourself at a disadvantage. The reason I say this, is because there is a thirty day time frame in which the credit bureaus have to respond to any dispute. If they do not respond within that thirty day time frame, the negative item must be removed. By you using the online dispute process that makes it easier on the credit bureaus because they don't have to perform a true investigation, which they don't do anyway, but you must leave a paper trail just in case you have to take legal action. The best way to deal with the credit bureaus is through the United States Postal Service. By using their online dispute system E-OSCAR, you have no proof of the dispute or a paper trail that certified the request was ever submitted. The credit bureaus online dispute system is set up in such a way that when you use it, their job becomes easier.

When the Fair Credit Reporting Act was revised by FACTA, they put in a section for "Expedited Dispute Resolution" section 611a (8), also known as the online dispute system. If you read this section, you will notice the following sentence:

"The agency shall not be required to comply with paragraphs 2, 6, and 7, with respect to that dispute, if they delete the trade line within 3 days."

Paragraph 2 is the part that requires the CRA to forward your dispute and all related documentation you provide to the creditor or company furnishing the information to the CRA

Paragraph 6 is the part that requires the CRA to provide you with written results of the investigation.

Paragraph 7 is the part that requires the CRA to provide you with the method of verification on request from the consumer.

The law is not specific enough and does not say permanently delete or suppress. Herein lays the problem. The credit reporting Agency (CRA) can "soft delete" a disputed trade line for 30 days and then the trade line can reappear when the creditor reports it again in the next 30-day cycle. This is due to the fact that the CRA's are not required to tell the creditor or collector that you disputed it at all thanks to "SHALL NOT BE REQUIRED TO COMPLY WITH PARAGRAPH 2." The credit bureaus can reject any dispute they like, especially if they determine it to be irrelevant or frivolous. They are supposed to conduct "reasonable" investigations also known as reinvestigation. When they reinvestigate a dispute they must review and consider all relevant information submitted by the consumer. How could this be possible, if a dispute is processed on-line and reduced to a three digit code? Unless you are very wealthy, most people cannot avoid having credit. At some point they will need to borrow money, buy a house or receive utilities in their name. Therefore, most Americans will be subjected to this web of credit entrapment.

After several minutes of watching the FBI enter my home and begin searching, I became frustrated, violated and most of all singled out. After all, I had been labeled a credit terrorist. I ran back to my car and decided that I was going to face the music. As I pulled up to my house and got out of the car, I was immediately arrested.

■

"Financial freedom will never come where ignorance exists."

— Corey P. Smith

Outsourcing America's Identity

There are so many ways the credit bureaus make money and they do it at a cost. Never forget that you are not a customer in the eyes of the credit bureaus, but you are profit when it comes to their annual financial projections. Now that may be hard for many people to understand, but what is not hard to understand is that money can buy almost anything even love no matter what part of the world you live. The customers are the banks and the credit bureaus make the most money from the services and abundance of information they provide to the banks. However, there was one sector of the credit world that was costing them more money than they wanted to spend and that was consumer disputes. The credit bureaus were spending $4.67 per consumer disputes prior to 2004 before the Fair and Accurate Credit Transaction Act was passed, but by 2005, they discovered that it was more cost effective to outsource consumer disputes overseas.

Equifax was the first credit bureau to experiment with outsourcing consumer disputes by using a company called ACS in Montego Bay, Jamaica. They initially reduced Equifax cost by $3.00 saving them millions of dollars despite the fact they were handing over very private information belonging to American citizens. Equifax also use vendors in Costa Rica and the Philippines. They are able to do all of this by using a company called INNASOURCE. INNASOURCE allows them to scan the images into an electronic format and then transfer via the internet. The other company in the

Philippines called DDC has helped Equifax reduce their cost even more by only charging them $0.57 per dispute with no limit on the number of disputes being processed. If you are wondering about TransUnion, they refuse to be left behind.

TransUnion uses a company called Intelenet located in Mumbai, India. TransUnion has the same blueprint as Equifax. Consumer disputes are scanned into electronic images and then transferred via TransUnion database known as CRONUS. Intelenet has direct access to the CRONUS database and can retrieve the customers' credit file as well. TransUnion cost to do all of this is about $0.49. The most frightening thing about all of this is foreign companies are not governed by US privacy laws. Remember, one of the fastest growing crimes is identity theft and credit bureaus spend plenty of money putting negative information in the media about victims of identity theft, but yet and still they have exposed millions of Americans personal information to possible identity thieves who may now target these foreign based companies as prey. In addition to credit bureaus making money off the consumer, they also make money off the banks too. You see any time the banks give the credit bureaus incorrect account information about a consumer they are charged $0.25 per infraction. Once again, the credit bureaus are making a profit off of mistakes, even the ones passed along to them by the banks. But, why would the banks even want to admit to providing incorrect information, especially if it was going to cost them money. You must consider the fact that account errors could be abundant because of how the banks submit the information to the credit bureaus. Each account is submitted on a daily basis along with millions of other accounts belonging to different consumers. The problem with this method is, all of the interactions are done via digital codes. What will happen once the banks decide they are losing too much money using this method and decide to outsource this process?

■

"The conversion of cash to plastic
is an unstoppable global trend."

— Philip J. Philliou

Tricks Credit Card Companies Play

Integrity is a strong word when you try to use it to define a person who is in need or trying to feed their family. Remember what Andrew Kahr said, "Is any bit of food too small to grab when you're starving and when there is nothing else in sight? I often tell people it's easy to have integrity when all of your wants and needs are met. But, try having integrity when you don't even know where your next meal is going to come from, not to mention when you have a wife and kids to feed. I have ask myself the question many times about my moral values or my integrity when it comes to dealing with creditors, i.e. banks, finance companies, collection agency and most of all the credit bureaus. Now, ask yourself the question, where should your integrity be when you are dealing with companies who do not know you, or the ones that are responsible for your livelihood. Many people do not realize that sometimes God will give you the tools to fight those individuals or companies that do not operate under the same definition that you have for the word integrity. Therefore, you should change your definition. I remember going to see the movie "Tower Heist" starring Eddie Murphy and Ben Stiller. There was a scene in the movie when Eddie Murphy, Ben Stiller and the rest of their team were captured and they were in the back of a police paddy wagon, with the guy who had stolen all of their life savings. The wealthy guy played by Jonathan Lewis, say's to Ben Stiller, "you are all expendable and can be easily replaced." You must remember this is the general philosophy of most of the political and corporate institutions. These institutions control the credit and financial well being of our country. So, I ask you again, "Do you know when you should have integrity?"

What is your definition of integrity? Let me give you a more realistic example of integrity. I make it a habit never to purchase a car under my personal credit, but always under a corporation. I have a friend by the name of Larry Mason, who always would tell me that I had a paranoid thought process. Well, Larry found himself like many others who were affected during these tough economic times with no job or home due to foreclosure.

Larry's car was repossessed by Ally bank. If you look at most car loans they will usually say something like, "Time is of the essence. In the event buyer defaults in any payment, seller shall have the right to declare all amounts due and payable and the right to reposes the property wherever the same maybe found with free right of entry, and to sell the same at public or private sale. Buyer shall remain liable for any deficiency." The word DEFICIENCY means, not only are you going to lose the car, but you will still owe the difference between what the car was bought for at the auction and whatever the balance was on your loan. Now, here is the true definition of integrity as defined by Ally bank. Not only did they repossess his car, sold it and placed a negative account on his credit report. They also 1099 him for the remaining balance of the vehicle along with all the other fees they could think of such as court and attorney's cost. For those of you who do not know, once a creditor gives you a 1099, it's like them giving you cash and you must report this to the IRS, which makes you liable for paying taxes on this debt. So now you are penalized twice. Once with bad credit and twice with having to pay taxes on something you no longer have. I have provided a copy of a 1099 filed on me by MACYS. I am providing this information because I want you to realize this is not make believe.

Wage and Income Transcript

Code "T" Expenses Incurred for Qualified Adoptions:	$0.00
Code "V" Income from exercise of non-statutory stock options:	$0.00
Code "AA" Designated Roth Contributions under a Section 401(k) Plan:	$0.00
Code "BB" Designated Roth Contributions under a Section 403(b) Plan:	$0.00
Code "CC" (For employer use only) - HIRE Exempt Wages and Tips:	$0.00
Third Party Sick Pay Indicator:	Unanswered
Retirement Plan Indicator:	Yes
Statutory Employee:	Not Statutory Employee

Form 1099-C Cancellation of Debt

Creditor:
Creditor's Federal Identification Number (FIN): 200307941
MACYS CORP SERV INC
PO BOX 8270
MASON, OH 45040-0000

Debtor:
Debtor's Identification Number: ~~XXX-XX-XXXX~~
COREY P SMITH
PO BOX 1752
CORDOVA, TN 38088-1752

Submission Type:	Original document
Account Number (Optional):	0000042239191562
Date Canceled:	10-05-2010
Property Fair Market Value:	0.00
Amount of Debt Canceled:	$1,085.00
Interest Forgiven Amount:	0.00
Bankruptcy Indicator:	Bankruptcy Not Indicated
Debt Description:	CREDIT CARD EXPENDITURE
Was borrower personally liable for repayment of the debt?	

This Product Contains Sensitive Taxpayer Data

However, there are other ways you can protect your car from the repo man, judgment creditors and other non-lien holders. You can place your own liens on the car.

You can get a friend or relative to give you a loan and secure it with a lien on your car. By doing this, the official lien-holder becomes just one among several entities with a lien on your car. My point is this, Larry was so busy trying to do the right thing and have integrity at the wrong time in regards to his credit that he left himself vulnerable to creditor's standards and definition of integrity. Obviously, Larry doesn't think that I have a paranoid thought process now. He actually considers me one of the smartest people he knows. I am telling you all of this because I would like you to understand that there are rules to this game of commerce and credit. If you are unaware of how to play the game, then you are not even in the game. My point is this, always try to purchase your vehicles under the name of a corporation, even if you have to incorporate a lemonade stand. This tactic of using a 1099 as a form of collection is becoming more popular among creditors and banks. I am going to give you very simple tricks that credit card companies play on consumers everyday and get richer with every trick.

The word trick is defined as an illusion or deception, which can be used for personal or commercial gain. The Card Act was put in place to help consumers from being manipulated into the many unfair games played by the credit card companies. But, banks have come up with many creative maneuvers to get around the Card Act. They have even beefed up their marketing strategies to introduce new products such as the professional cards now being offered to many customers. These professional cards are just like corporate or commercial credit cards that are not covered under the new Card Act. Another trick being played on consumers to help make up for revenue lost due to the new Card Act is the Rebate-Card. Credit card companies used to raise rates on customers who were less than 60 days late on their existing balances, but all of that changed with the new Card Act. This is the main reason for the rebate card. Rebate cards are not governed by the Card Act, and creditors can increase the rates any time they get ready. Tricks are like jigsaw puzzles you just have to pay attention long enough to figure them out. I once heard a story about a boy who wanted his father to play catch with him. I have heard this story told many different ways, but the meaning behind it is priceless. The boy asked his father, "Dad can you play catch with me in the front yard?" The father replied, "After I put this puzzle of the world together." The boy waited for a couple of hours and returned and asked his father once more. The father replied, "If you can put this puzzle of the world together, I will play catch with you." And so, the father left the boy alone for almost an hour before he returned. When the father returned, the boy had finished putting together the puzzle of the world. The father was amazed to say the least, and he asked his son, "How did you figure the puzzle out so fast?" The boy replied, "Dad I looked on the opposite side of the instructions, and there was a picture of a man's face, and so I just put the man's face together."

The point to this story is that sometimes, the key to all puzzles are staring us right in the face, but we over look it because of the simplicity of most situations. The reason we feel this way is that we have been trained to accept things for face value. Like I said before, "there is no blueprint to tell us exactly where our success or financial freedom lies. So we must figure out who we are and what we love to do as well as identifying what our talents may be in life." I have provided you with a list of tricks that credit card companies play on us as customers all in the name of profit. One thing that you must understand about credit, is that two million credit reports are ordered each day, two billion pieces of information are added to credit files each month and your credit report is updated at least five times a day on an average. If you couple all of this with the many tricks that credit card companies put in place to trap consumers into bogus contracts and outrageous fees and not to mention the ever-present identity protection services being offered to anyone with a credit report.

What you get is a billion dollar industry that preys on the poor. Also, remember that fraud is necessary. The reason I say this is because the credit bureaus create stories and statistics as well. They allow some identity theft for the purpose of making money. They use information to make people nervous and fearful that they somehow will become victims of irreversible identity theft.

I have listed several tricks that you should be aware of before you deal with any credit card issuer.

Sometimes they will post your payment late, even if they

received it on time. The reason they do this is that they can charge you a late fee. Sometimes they will change your due date. By doing this, it will cause you to be late on your payment therefore, you can be charged a late fee or your interest rate can be raised. If you are a person who does not use your credit card a certain number of times, they can charge you a penalty fee, for not using your credit card enough.

For some people who are fortunate enough to get credit, they are offered credit card protection in case the card is lost or stolen. The other offer is insurance in case you loose your job and cannot make payments. Stay away from either of these offers. Some credit card companies will automatically increase your limit so that you can spend more. Remember the more you spend, the greater the chances of profit for the credit card company.

Credit card companies are now charging fees when you cancel your credit card. Remember to never close an account that has a balance. The best thing to do is close the account after you have paid it off.

Credit card companies are now charging a fee to customers who carry a high balance. Try to avoid mandatory arbitration because if there is a dispute, you may have to give up your rights to your day in the court room. Your only choice will be mandatory arbitration. The commission charged for the amount of credit card use outside the United States is much higher than charges made within the United States. Credit card companies might charge a foreign transaction fee on any international transaction when they have to convert currency.

This might happen to you when you are making an internet purchase with a company that processes payments outside the United States.

Some creditors such as Macy's and Capitol One do not report their customer's credit limits. When the creditor does not report the consumer's credit limit, the credit bureaus use the "highest balance charged" as a proxy for the limit. An example of this would be: If you use $400 of a $1000 limit that is reported correctly, the scoring formulas would figure your "credit utilization" at 40%, and that would be OK! The problem is when your limit is not reported and the highest balance you ever charged would be $400, it appears as though you are using 100% of your available credit and that's BAD! So the best thing that you can do is keep your balance at zero. Not reporting your credit limit would make sense, if you had an American Express card.

Credit card companies will also try to make more money off you by charging a finance charge on your balance. They will usually do this by decreasing your grace period. That is why you should always mail your payment off as soon as you receive your billing statement.

Many credit card companies charge card holders an annual fee, if you don't charge a certain amount each year. They came up with this because credit card companies use to charge inactivity fee to customers who did not use their card that often, but the government stop them from using this practice. Therefore, the best things you can do is try and pay your card off each time you make a charge.

There is something called "fee harvester." These are subprime credit cards that charge upfront processing fees even before they open an account for you. Most of the time this happens with secured credit cards. That is why you should always read the credit card disclosure of any credit card offer.

Sometimes a consumers due date may fall on a holiday or Sunday, and credit card companies will charge a late payment fee, if they receive a payment after either one of these days. This is a violation of the Credit Card Act, because it states credit card companies cannot charge a late fees, when credit card payments are received the next business day after a weekend or holiday.

Another trick played by credit card companies is the "Cash Back." The truth is cash back comes with certain stipulations, such as shopping at stores you don't even like and there is a cap. This means your cash back is only good, if the amount you get back is below a certain limit. Most of the times you do not even get the money back at all. This also is true for Reward Points as well. Reward points are only a way to make you spend more money.

Always beware of low minimum payments because the lower the monthly payments are, the longer the loan repayment period will be. You will be paying more interest on the credit card.

Remember to pay attention to your grace period. By law, you are entitled to 20 or 25 days grace period after you receive your bill. The problem is that credit card companies are quietly doing away with the grace period without the customer knowing it. As a result, when the customer slips on his or her monthly bill, they will be charged interest rates from day one.

Have you ever thought about why credit card companies sometimes let you go over your limit? It is because by approving your over limit charge they can charge you an over the limit penalty. That is interest on the outstanding balance and increases your interest rate on your credit card. Sometimes they can accomplish this by decreasing your credit limit and as a result you are over your credit limit due to the decrease. Credit card companies will also try to increase the interest rate on your credit card by using your credit score as a reason. This is known as the Universal Default. An example of this would be your credit score dropping due to a missed car or mortgage payment.

The 0% introductory offer may seem like the greatest offers on credit cards, but the truth is it may hurt you in the long run, if you do not pay attention to the fine print. The credit card companies will trick you with words. What I mean by this is, they may be able to increase your interest rate instantly, if you get a high balance while still in the introductory period. The fine print may also state that some credit card customers may get the 0% interest rate for a year and others for six months. So always consider time frames as well.

The next time you consider applying for or accepting a credit card, remember that credit was indeed created for the poor. Poor people are trained by society to want the "good life," but society will not provide the poor the necessary tools needed to fulfill these socially induced wants. Poor people have no cash, no savings and no job security. All these factors contribute to the business of credit. The business of credit is so complex that it sometimes confuses even the most intelligent poor person. Even smart consumers never stop to think about the true cost of what they are receiving on credit or length of the contract. Credit is only profitable for the rich and an illusion for the poor, simply because credit is more expensive for those who cannot pay for it in the end. Because the fact of the matter is, if you need credit and you have no cash, then there is no end. Whether it is bad or good credit, whatever you needed credit for will never survive beyond the cost of receiving it on CREDIT!

My point is this. If you are predictable then you can easily be fooled. Credit operates in a cycle, just like the weather. That just means any and all persons are bound to slip up at some point and the people who create these algorithms know this probability. This serves the people who extend credit all power because they already know how to set you up. Remember when I stated earlier that credit bureaus plant seeds of fear to get consumers to buy into certain products such as credit protection services. Think about this, if the protection of American consumer's credit was so important, why the credit bureaus would outsource their credit monitoring services offshore where there are no laws to govern the privacy or protection of your credit. If you read any of the service agreements and the privacy policy for any of these credit monitoring sites, such as True Credit, you will see it mentions that consumer's information may be shared with third parties. Many people have no idea credit bureaus started outsourcing their credit reporting services offshore for the purpose of saving money and staying competitive back in 2003. One year before the FACT ACT.

■

"Though the process impoverishes many,
it actually enriches some."

— John Maynard Keynes

Appetite for Credit

Many people do not think about all the cell phone calls they make or when they use their debit or credit card. What about that flight you booked, website you visited, your school records, doctors visit or even that discount card you got from the grocery store. What if, all this information was being collected and stored in a database. Well it is being collected and stored everyday using a process known as data mining. This process is so useful that even the grocery stores have begun to use it in ways that you could never imagine. Even more disturbing, the credit bureaus are helping them cash in by selling your personal information. In the early 90's grocery stores began introducing purchase tracking programs, better known as reward, discount, loyalty and frequent shopper cards. This purchase tracking program was patterned after the format used by the credit bureaus to gather information about consumers.

The grocery stores were tricking people into believing they were receiving discounts but secretly gathering longitudinal information on consumer purchases and eating habits. Along with millions of other records, the information is stored in an enormous "data warehouse" where it is analyzed in detail. Today all of this information gathered through grocery store discount cards are being bought and used by insurance companies, credit card issuers, law enforcement and healthcare facilities. Ask yourself, what is more important than food? Nothing everything else is a want. Grocery store discount cards are just another retail surveillance tactic used by creditors. Remember, that most people are coerced by fear. It is no different with grocery shopping. People believe that unless they have a discount or loyalty card they're not saving money, when in fact it's just the opposite and they are giving up valuable personal information in the process. In the world of credit this is called consumer negligence. Meaning you gave your personal information away to be used against you.

You are probable thinking, I didn't give my social security number or date of birth, so how can they do anything with just a name and address? EASY! A computer process known as "re-identification" can allow creditors, bill collectors or anyone who buys this information from the grocery stores to re-attach names and addresses to "anonymous' records, even after all the identifying information has been removed. Think about whenever you ordered your credit report and they ask you for your date of birth or zip code. Re-identification works the same way. It combines the "anonymous" information with outside information such as a zip code or date of birth. The sad thing about all of this is privacy policies mean nothing when it comes to your personal information being shared. Most companies, especially credit bureaus have a right to give your information to other brands in their family of products or "partner" companies and remember the credit bureaus own more than you know. Keep in mind that information is not always power, it can sometimes be your enemy.

President Bill Clinton once said, "More than 95% of the people that are in the United States at any given time are in the computers of companies that mail junk mail and you can look for patterns there." He was referring to "suspicious behavior." The reason why this statement is so important is because not only do banks, credit card issuers and credit bureaus use this phrase to frustrate most honest consumers, it is also used by law enforcement agencies. The catch to this is they use credit reports, purchasing behaviors, and healthcare records with names and addresses to build detailed data about you the consumer. You may be thinking, "Well I can just use fictitious or anonymous information when I fill out applications for supermarket discount cards or department store applications when I want the discount although I know my credit is bad." This will soon come to an end with "document fraud" being the new buzz word in law enforcement and politics since September 11, 2001. In addition, it carries a maximum 15 year prison sentence. You must consider the fact that every Visa and MasterCard transaction around the world goes through a US server at some point. This is a valuable source of data, therefore law enforcement and intelligence agencies routinely use financial records, including credit reports and data from your grocery store discount card as part of their investigation. In case you did not know, telecom companies get paid to respond to FBI requests and the major credit card networks have streamlined processes through which they can respond to law enforcement request as well as get paid.

Any person can be identified with the least amount of information using what is known as geodemographic, psychographic and purchasing characteristics. The problem is the people being identified and analyzed the most are poor people. I was once told that poor people are expendable, especially the elderly. Wells Fargo bank proved this idealism to be true. In 1998, they discovered that most of their money was being lost on older customers who were on social security, so unknowingly to the customers, they raised their checking and overdraft fees for all of their customers on social security. You see banks will always view poor people as being the "least profitable." However, less fortunate will always be profitable to those companies that extend credit not cash. The reason I wanted to include this section on grocery store loyalty and discount cards being used to gather information about people is because sometimes people will not do things because they are asked. There are four ways to get people to do things you want besides asking. They are lying, stealing, fear and the biggest is by way of hope. Who do you think is more dangerous a robber of con-man? If you said robber, you were wrong. You see, when a robber acts you know exactly what he is up to, but a con-man plays with your mind and emotions. That emotion is HOPE! Most people can be persuaded to do anything with the hope of being better off.

Right now the grocery and health industry are the best avenues to gather information from people without them knowing it. Already a microchip known as "Health Passport Card" is being issued to people on welfare in three cities in the United States. The microchip is used to store and retrieve information on welfare recipients. It is also required to purchase groceries under the Women, Infants and Children (WIC) program. In addition to that, it links food purchase information with health and immunization records. What does all of this mean? It means that eventually the identification for credit, food purchases, health records may require all citizens to have a sub dermal computer chip implant, such as the veri-chip produced by Applied Digital Solutions. When the government and private corporations can completely persuade people that all of this is done in the best interest of privacy and freedom, it will give them omniscient powers of observation over the people.

■

"Government is an evolutionary thing and has only one direction to evolve, towards more control."

— Allen Leigh

Speed of Light Credit

I really struggled when trying to explain the blueprint behind the RFID microchip and its significance as it relates to credit and a cashless society. This concept is very simple but may still be too space age for many people to believe it can ever be possible. Remember, that anything introduced to mainstream media or the public is kept in secrecy from ten to thirty years. You will be propagandized by the media, government and popular culture into believing this is all for your own good, your own safety, even that it's cool, but this is a system of control and nothing more. Remember in the introduction when I said that I would explain the true meaning behind VISA. If you look at a Visa credit card you see three previous world empires represented. "VI" is the number 6 in the Roman numerals, "S" is the Stigma in the Greek culture whose value is 6, and the "A" in the Babylonian culture is 6 i.e., VISA=666! Please understand that mathematical impossibilities are not conspiracies, but can in fact predict the possibilities of the future. In the book of revelations Chapter 13, verse 16-17, "He (the beast) forced everyone, small and great, rich and poor, free and slave, to receive a mark in his right hand or in his forehand, so that no one could buy or sell unless he had the mark, which is the name of the beast or the number of his name. There are two reasons why this bible verse carries a prophetic power that cannot be defined as a coincidence, but in fact a conspiracy created 3000 years before Christ. Part of the revelation states, "to receive a mark in his right hand," and the other, "the number of his name." Now, in order for you to understand why receiving a mark in his right hand is so important, you must know something about RFID chips. However, "the number of his name," can easily be deciphered as your social security number. Ask yourself the question how could any human being who lived thousands of years ago, could ever know that an RFID chip would exist or that a social security number would be "THE NUMBER OF OUR NAME."

To explore this theory further, it is believed the ancient Chaldeans, had a numerological technique that was used during the Babylonian empire that can be translated to the English alphabet today. In their system each succeeding letter of the alphabet was equal to 6 more than the one before it. If you translate that to our system, A would equal 6; B would equal 12, and so on. I have provided a chart to help you understand this technique.

A	6	E	30	I	54	M	78	Q	102	U	126
B	12	F	36	J	60	N	84	R	108	V	132
C	18	G	42	K	66	O	90	S	114	W	138
D	24	H	48	L	72	P	96	T	120	X	144

Remember, I explained the number of his name could be interpreted as your social security number. Let's see if we can use this numerological technique to calculate "social security number" aka SSNUMBER.

S   19x6=114

S   19x6=114

N 14x6=84

U 21x6=126

M 13x6=78

B 2x6= 12

E 5x6=30

R 18x6=108

      +666

One thing that must be understood about our global economy is everything is commerce and not a barter system. The notion that 666 represent the mark of the beast also implies that the mark might actually be associated with credit and we must have some type of credit to be recognized in business. All this points to the RFID chip. THINK, "No one may buy or sell except one who has the mark or name of the beast, or the number of his name, and his number is 666," Revelation 13:17-18. Buying, Selling and making purchases can be linked to credit. I will take it a step further. UPC bar codes were introduced in the 1970's. Today, almost every product we buy has a UPC or Universal Product Code imprinted on it. All UPC codes have the number 666 encoded within them. Bar codes, in general, are made up of lines of various widths and distances apart. Each numeral has a two-line code. The code for the number six is two thin lines, a short distance apart. The "Control Codes" on the far left, middle, and right of all UPC codes contain the number 666. Look at the example of a UPC bar code below.

The interpretation of the Book of Revelation, which indicates that the number of the beast is required for all business transactions. Most people have been taught that the number 666 is associated with the return of the antichrist. What they don't understand is that 666 "mark of the beast" is really a representation of credit and a global economy controlled by microchips. Think about how most of the buying and selling today is geared towards using your credit or debit cards, or better yet over the internet. When I speak about credit and the credit bureaus and how much control they have over our lives, there are many pieces to a puzzle that must be considered. Why do you think credit card companies and credit bureaus push you to do everything on line? The sixth letter of the Hebrew alphabet is "waw" or "vav." Its closest relation in English is the letter "w."

This ubiquitous acronym "www" as in www.myfreecreditreport.com, can also be interpreted as the number of the beast.

The RFID microchip is the size of a rice grain that can be inserted into the right hand. It can one day be used to pay for groceries, unlock doors, activate alarms, and turn on lights and most of all used as credit. All with the wave of your hand. The RFID chip has been around for more than twenty years. It was first used to keep track of race horses, cats, and dogs. In 2002, the Verichip Corporation of Delray Beach, Florida received FDA approval as a Class 2 medical device. Verichip Corporation signed a medical distribution agreement on November 10, 2004, with Henry Schein one of the largest distributors of healthcare products in North American and European markets. Now keep in mind that TransUnion owns First Health Group and back in 1995 Equifax and AT&T issued a press release stating they were joining to form a company called Healthcare Information Service Group. All of this merging between communication, credit and healthcare companies created the perfect blueprint for a cashless society. Verichip's ultimate goal is an implanted chip that links to an online database containing all your medical records, credit history and your social security number. The catch to this is the world's financial institutions have announced their goal is to move towards a CASHLESS SOCIETY. Simply put, their goal is to conduct all monetary exchange by microchip technology and electronic currency. The reason why this is possible is because the RFID chip consist of a miniature antenna and chip containing a 16-digit identification number that can be scanned by an RFID reader. Once verified the number is used to unlock a database file, whether it is a medical record or payment information. This is already being done with credit cards now. The only difference is that the 16 digit identifying number is not implanted in humans. What is even more amazing is that, depending on the application the RFID microchip can be read at a distance of four inches up to 30 feet.

In order to understand the true meaning of what this RFID microchip stands for and how it relates to credit and monetary transactions, you must pay attention to the blueprint for cashless society. First, there is a company called MONDEX, which provides cashless systems and has already franchised in over twenty major countries. Their system is designed using Smart Card technology that employs microchips concealed in plastic cards which stores electronic cash, and identification information. Most of the smart card's early development happened in France while involving companies from all over the world. Smart card developments eventually lead to Visa's super smart card and subsequently Visa Cash and Mondex cards. The concept of memory card or smart cards started in France. Simply stated, the idea was embed a computer chip that contained information about the holder of the card or value of some sort, make it secure, and then being able to retrieve this information via the chip's contacts on one side. The concept of the smart card was invented and patented in France by Roland Moreno. In 1976, Moreno demonstrated the first use of a smart card for electronic payments. His concepts and patents were the catalyst for smart card advancement in France, where unlike the United States and other countries the phone system and service was notoriously poor. This technology is currently being designed using what is called SET protocols, which stands for Secure Electronic Transaction. These SET protocols will display the SET MARK.

MON-DEX is a compound word that stands for monetary and dexter. If you look in Webster's dictionary, it will define these words as:

Monetary- pertaining to money

Dexter- belonging to or located on the right hand

SET- the Egyptian God

Now here is where it gets interesting. MasterCard bought 51% shares of Mondex. Remember I told you that MasterCard's ultimate goal is to have a cashless economic system. Mondex is associated with a company called Applied Digital Solutions (ADS). Applied Digital Solutions is on the NASDAQ and traded as a high tech company, that has a patent right to a miniature digital transceiver, which it nicknamed "Digital Angel." The transceiver is versatile because it can receive and send data, which can be implanted in humans. It can provide a tamper proof means of identification. Now consider what "Digital Angel" stands for when it is broken down. Webster defines digital as: of or pertaining to a digit or finger and angel as: a spiritual being believed to act as a messenger or agent of God. This is all a perfect fit for Mondex's innovative payment system that combines the best features of traditional cash with the convenience of electronic payment.

People with the implant can buy with no cash, credit cards or debit cards. A simple implant chip is all that is needed to conduct business. This cashless system created by MONDEX was created in 1993 by London bankers Tim Jones and Graham Higgins of NATWEST/COUTTS, the personal bank of Britain's Royal family. The bio-chip invented to compliment the cashless system was developed by Dr. Carl Sanders, former Engineer of Electronics for Motorola. The bio-chip is used for global use in humans for economic and identification purposes, and contains a rechargeable lithium battery. They discovered that if the chip would be in a card, they would encounter serious problems. The chip could be cut and information could be changed or falsified. The value could be manipulated, stolen, or lost. In the end, real money will become obsolete in the world economy.

Motorola spent millions of dollars to find the best place for the bio-chip. YOU GOT IT! The right hand. By placing it on the back of the right hand, the chip can only be removed by way of surgery. If it is removed other than surgery, the small capsule will burst and the individual would be contaminated by the lithium and the chemical in the micro-bacteria. At that point, the GPS system would detect if it was removed and would alert the authorities. They are rolling it out right now and they are making it seem like its fun and for your own good. Keith Bolton, the chief technology officer for Applied Digital Solutions stated, "When people are trying to regain their peace of mind, they're more open to new approaches." Now think about how many people live their life in search of hope and trying to find a peace of mind, but can't because those in control of worldwide economic development and social progress create a matrix of poverty that cannot be overcome.

I will leave you with this thought. Think back as far as you can remember when you began going to school. You were always taught to raise your right hand, write with your right hand, and walk on the right side of the hall. Much of this stems from religious superstition. The left hand and the left side were called the sinister side by religion. This belief derived from the misinterpretations of biblical scriptures regarding (Ephesians 1:19-21), Jesus being seated at the right hand of God. So the practice of making children use their right hands in school was influenced by this belief. To sit at ones right hand means a place of authority, a place of honor and ruler ship.

It was Lord Byron who said it first, I believe: "Tis strange, but true; for truth is always strange; Stranger than fiction." I say this because all of this information may seem far-fetched to many who read this book, but carefully consider the words and symbolism used to move our world towards a Cashless Society. The term "mark of the beast" and "666" has great meaning. The "Mark" from the mark of the beast was termed this way: mark:charagma; from Greek Charax meaning to stake down into or " stick into"__ like to stick into the hand like an Implant. The number 666 is the Greek phrase Chi Xi Sigma, meaning to stick or prick, or mark incised or punched for the recognition of ownership. But we are being tricked into thinking that the right hand always represent honor. Seriously pay attention to what I am about to say in the next paragraph.

The industry name for the advanced smartcard developed by GEMPLUS and the US DOD (Department of Defense) is MARC (Multi-Technology Automated Reader Card). The code name for its development was "TESSERA." A tessera was the Roman insignia of ownership placed on their slaves, which if removed would result in the slave being branded with a mark. Remember what happens when a bio-chip is removed without surgery? In November 1996, an agreement was made by GEMPLUS to supply smartcards for the global implementation of MONDEX. AT&T/Lucent Technologies purchased the franchise for MONDEX USA. This company's former address is listed below.

Lucent Technologies Inc.

666 5TH Ave.

New York, NY. 10103-0001

Remember when I said, anything introduced to main stream media or the public is kept is secrecy from ten to thirty years. Simply put, the application is buying and selling, the technology is implantable and the plans are global. Remember, "No man might buy or sell," and we are the tools of rich men behind the scenes. Nothing more than intellectual prostitutes. Our talents, our possibilities and our lives are all the property of other men.

■

"We were making the future," he said,
"and hardly any of us troubled to
think what future we were making.
And here it is!"

— The Sleeper Awakes, H.G. Wells

Education of Debt

There are many great mysteries that we as human beings are still astonished by on a daily basis. I often find myself day dreaming about life and death. I wonder why there are some people who achieve fame and fortune. I wonder why are there so many tricks and traps put in place to keep us in bondage. And then I think about this quote. "When the suffer begins to think, the thinker will begin to suffer." But what does that really mean? How can the suffer ever begin to think when his thinking is controlled by a system that creates all the rights and wrongs in our lives. Well, one thing that I figured out is that we are all free will beings created by one GOD and one GOD only! Any person is free to think and use his education to come to a conclusion. Any person can use his education to rationalize or make logic of this world, but true education is birth through wisdom that is only acquired by way of experience, which then evolves into knowledge. Simply put, a true education has no blueprint. I once read somewhere that, " People who admire our school institution usually admire networking in general and have an easy time seeing its positive side, but they over look its negative aspect: networks, even good ones, drain the vitality from communities and families. They provide mechanical ("by-the-numbers") solutions to human problems, when a slow organic process of self-awareness, self discovery, and cooperation is what is required if any solution is to stick." Think back to when you were a child and someone asked you, "What do you want to be when you grow up?" Whatever your response was to the question didn't matter. What did matter was that you believed that you could be whatever you dreamed. But, the problem is education got in the way of our dreams and we were educated on how to be afraid, insecure and obedient. What proceeded that was the inability to dream and use our inner genius.

If you ask anybody, what is wrong with the educational system in America? They will tell you that it is f@!*#d UP! But it's not. In actuality it is doing exactly what it was designed to do dumb you down. In John Gattos book "Dumbing Us Down," he states, "School teaches confusion, class position, indifference, emotional and intellectual dependency, conditional self esteem, and surveillance. All these lessons are prime training for permanent underclass, people deprived forever of finding the center of their own special genius." We have been tricked into debt by education as well. The educational system was designed to create a system to liberate people through schooling, but lock them into conformity for life. From the time kids enter kindergarten, they are taught that they must have good grades in order to attend college, which ensures a good job. They are also taught, if they don't go to college and get a degree, then life maybe a dead end. Most people believe that college is a necessity and by the time they reach high school, students already believe in the psychology that college will guarantee them a successful life. None of this is true. I can truly say that I learned nothing in college that has helped me achieve the success I have obtained. As a matter of fact, if I had to do it all over again I probably would not have even graduated high school. But that is the beauty of wisdom, only time can capture it. How many times have you found yourself saying, "If I knew then, what I know now? That's funny because the future is now.

Let me explain. This book is about the conspiracies of credit. The biggest conspiracy is education. Remember, when the suffer begins to think. The suffers thinking is always controlled by the thinker. People are taught to accept bondage, and this is done through education. Now think about it? What bigger bondage is there besides debt? There is none. In the 1970's, the government created Sallie Mae, but by the 1990's Sallie Mae had turned itself into a private for-profit corporation. Once Sallie Mae became a private for-profit corporation, it then lobbied Congress into cancelling all consumer rights, when it came to student loans. That included the statute of limitations, the right to bankruptcy and the right to refinance. It is almost impossible to get out of paying your student loans, but there are two ways you can possibly defend yourself. One way is to change the withholding on your paycheck so that at the end of year you owe taxes. What difference does it make, if your taxes are going to be taken anyway? The other way is by trying to establish some unusual medical condition. You see, the average student graduates $20,000 in debt and $100,000, if they want a graduate degree. I guess when you look at it; they become educated indentured servants of a system that obligates them to payment for a lifetime. They also don't realize they are nothing more than intellectual prisoners and never question the collegiate mythologies, they have been taught at such an expensive price. College is a tradition that is passed down from generation to generation, but stop and think, it's also a tradition of debt passed down as well.

What many people do not know is that student loans are bundled and sold in the financial market to investors, just like mortgages and credit card debt. What's even funnier is that student loans are not based on credit worthiness, because they are guaranteed by the federal government, but you will pay dearly in the end. Remember, "when the suffer begins to think." Does any of this makes sense given the fact that student loans are high risk financial products and colleges know this and so they act like for profit corporations, merging with banks, credit card companies and book publishers to trick students into buying over priced textbooks. To add insult to injury a tenured professor can increase his income by making his overpriced textbook a course requirement, which he has authored under contract with the publisher. The same book may cost $300, but are only worth $20 once the semester is over. Sometimes publishers will even revise the book, which means students have to buy the newly revised copy per the professor teaching the course.

Early, I stated, "that college did not help me and I probably would have dropped out of high school, if I had to do it all over again." My reasoning behind this was because high school did not teach me any entrepreneur skills, nor did college. I figured out that if someone would have taught me about credit, banking, business and real estate, wealth would have come faster. I could have used the time I wasted in college to work and make mistakes investing and trying to build wealth as opposed to wasting years creating debt. Instead, what is happening now is that colleges and universities are profiting off of student loans. First of all, government guaranteed loans mean profit for the banks and the lenders that get paid to service these loans. You see student loans are "Asset Backed Securities."

The servicers are basically third parties the government uses to repackage and bundle the student loans to auction off to investors. These investors are mainly banks or hedge funds. It is mainly the debt being traded as an asset. This is good for investors because the student loans are backed by the federal government, which means a lifetime loan that will never be paid back and can never be discharged in bankruptcy. The bottom line is the loans never lose value, because the government covers 98 or 99% of the value. Think about this, student loans or college tuition didn't decline in price even during the recession or mortgage crunch.

College is almost impossible to afford without taking out a student loan, but the psychology of getting a college degree is so powerful that you have the parents of college athletes who have the opportunity to earn millions in the pros make statements like, "I want him to come back and get his degree." Really, for what? Consider the fact that college coaches and universities are paid millions, but athletes who don't make it as pros are left with debt and an education they can't use. A college degree is declining in value because of the economy and the number of jobs available, but tuition is continuing to rise. Student loan debt is an estimated $ 1 trillion dollars. There is another problem that you see being advertised on TV everyday trying to convince would be students the opportunity to come and get an unaffordable education. Schools like the University of Phoenix, Strayer, DeVry, ITT and Everest are for profit colleges that pay for commercials claiming college graduates earn more money, than those without a degree. This is nothing more than an advertising scam. They collect billions of dollars every year from the federal government in the form of student loans. They target those most likely to receive federal student loans: low income students, immigrants, students of color and other nontraditional types of students. Basically they will allow anyone who meets these criterias to enroll in school, with the help of a college representative, better known as a sales associate. I want you to think about this statement made by a former for-profit-recruiter. She stated, "The pain funnel was used to demoralize potential applicants by discussing their life's shortcomings in order to have them enroll, where their life would improve. Such techniques are both predatory and very successful. She went on to say, "Students would enroll with the expectation that if they spend enough money, whether through savings or student loans, their problems would be solved, but for a large percentage of students who enrolled, this was simply not the case." Now think about that the next time you watch one of those commercials claiming college graduates earn three times more than high school graduates. It is time for you the suffer to begin to think and examine what the most successful people in the world did to accomplish their goals. Three of the richest men in the world all dropped out of college and they are Bill Gates, Warren Buffet, and Mark Zuccelberg. Remember, the most useful information is always

116

given to the wealthy and privileged first. So PAY ATTENTION! I will end this chapter with a quote from Ayn Rand, who said, "Wealth is the product of man's capacity to think."

■

"Banking institutions are like standing armies."

— Thomas Jefferson

End of Cash

I have just returned home from New York and I'm lying in the bed with my wife, when the doorbell rings. This came as a surprise because no one comes to visit us without prior notice. So, I jumped up and looked out of the window. To my surprise I see these cars that appear to be government vehicles. This was very shocking because I had no idea why they would be coming to my house, especially given the fact, my utilities were in an alias and the deed was registered under a trust. I answered the door and it's the Secret Service. I noticed one of them had a picture of me in his hand. They ask that infamous question, I have heard so many times, "are you Corey Smith?" I respond by saying, "Yes, how may I help you?" They explained to me that they are not there to arrest me, but simply had some questions they wanted to ask about a check I had deposited in the bank. They told me the bank was suspicious and screaming Fraud! Fraud! Fraud! They were extremely friendly, but of course that was all a part of the coke and a smile routine. This peaked my curiosity because I wanted to know why the Secret Service would be interested in a check that I deposited in my name. As they began to talk, one of them pulled out some credit reports and all of them had my name at the top, but a different social security number. Immediately, I knew this was more than about a check I deposited.

I immediately stop the Secret Service agent and said to him, "listen if you know me, than you know this is not my first time around the block. So don't bullshit me and I won't bullshit you."

After that one of the agents explains to me that they simply want to know how did I set the credit files up and keep them separate. They also told me that they had spoken to the credit bureaus and the Social Security Administration and they knew that the social security numbers had been issued, but didn't know who they belonged to at the present time. At that moment I knew they were lying to me about whatever it was they truly wanted to know. I also thought to myself, it's amazing how law enforcement officials can lie to you in efforts to trick you, but if you lie to them, the result is you can be arrested. I remember this quote from a book called "Dumbing Us Down" by John Gatto. It says, "Do not destroy or kill your enemies. Educate them for they are more valuable to you alive than dead."

They were my enemies, simply because their goal was to trick me, steal information from me and take me away from my family, but wanted me to believe they were my friends in the process. It all begin to make sense, it was the bank that had put a flag on my name. Banks treat all large cash deposits as "suspicious transactions" and they will cover themselves by immediately reporting cash loaded customers to the authorities. Most people do not believe in conspiracy and that's sad because most of the things that hinder the growth of poor people are very real, but given the appearance of being just another conspiracy. Remember, I told you one of the agents stated, "Someone at the bank was screaming FRAUD, FRAUD, and FRAUD! Well, that wasn't true. In actuality cash has no provenance. Meaning, unlike checks or credit cards it is very difficult in cash transactions to associate a purchaser with a purchase, or a purchase with other purchases. So that makes audit trails expensive as well as cash. That is one of the reasons credit cards and grocery loyalty cards are so valuable. Remember, I talked about the RFID chips and all of its capabilities. An RFID chip can also be fitted into banknotes, so as to identify each note uniquely as it passes within range of a sensor. If you don't believe me look up this commercial on YouTube by IBM called future shopper. The authorities would like for you to believe its purpose is to combat counterfeiting and to identify money transfers between suspicious parties. RFID readers can identify every time notes are passed to or from a bank. RFID readers will identify and record them and link this data with the person who presents or receives them. But, could it be my three names presented a problem, which made the Secret Service suspicious. You see the US Patriot Act and the Proceeds of Crime Act have all been cleverly rushed through. Politicians and government agencies have learned the lesson of the successful 1931 conviction of Al Capone by the US Treasury. If you can't catch a criminal in the act, then "follow the money" instead.

Most people believe in banks and that's good, because ultimately money is backed by nothing but your own confidence, habits and faith. A form of faith as powerful and essential to your everyday life, as any religious belief. The coming of digital money will make this plain to everyone eventually. You see, digital money is perfect money, flawless money, and intangible money. It is money that can't be scuffed, worn, dirty or perhaps lost. It is networked money, point of sale money, money on a card and money on a computer. It is money that weighs nothing and moves at the speed of light. It is information, something that money has always been. Most of all it is information about value and wealth. It can tell you who is rich and who is poor. Have you ever realized that the IRS is probably the one institution as it relates to money, that you can never escape? I mean consider this fact; eliminating cash would empower the IRS even more. Right now computer databases keep track of every magazine you buy, every bus you ride, every hamburger you eat, every piece of grocery you purchase and every video you rent from the red box. This network of information that is being created can follow the trail of all you're spending. It enables the banks, credit bureaus, and government to become more omniscient. In the credit business, information is power and your spending habits, your likes and dislikes are valuable to marketers. Most of our economic life is already networked in every check; every credit card payment and every telephone call exist in a computer somewhere. If you don't believe me, think about the last time you ordered something on Amazon. You probably received an email from them later advertising a similar product as the one you previously purchased. Remember that cash is expensive and credit card companies have realized that their products are no longer about credit, but rather about convenient payment for goods and services. Do not forget, I told you MasterCard owns 51% of Mondex. Mondex has noticed that cash changes hands 300 billion times a year in the United States alone, and they want their cut. Many of you do not realize that smart phones, smart cars and smart whatever was just a way to introduce the beginning of the end of cash.

■

"The money power preys upon the nation in times of peace and conspires against it in times of adversity. It denounces as public enemies, all who question its methods or throw light upon its crime."

— Abraham Lincoln

Conclusion

I have just landed in Los Angeles, California, and the weather is beautiful and a sense of happiness has come over me, as it usually does whenever I come to Los Angeles. As I get off the plane I think to myself about all the ups and downs I have been through over the last several years. At one point, I felt as if my life was a failure and I was not one of those people who are blessed with a special gift. I mean all I ever wanted to do was provide a comfortable life for me and my family, but the one thing I could not see was the way I tried to obtain wealth. I was chasing money and not pursuing what made me happy. I have heard so many successful and wealthy people talk about following your heart and doing what makes you happy and the rest will follow. As I am headed to baggage claim I see a Forbes magazine with JAY Z on the front cover. It's amazing how someone like JAY Z could accomplish just as much as Donald Trump, but do it with less resources. After, I purchase the magazine and continue to get my luggage; I begin to consider the irony of a person like JAY Z who obtained wealth by doing what he loved to do as opposed to a person once described by B.C Forbes, who was the creator of Forbes magazine. He once stated, "A rich American, intellectually brilliant, but without mental or financial scruple, recently died. He was sore, sour, bitter. His sole concern in life was to leave a certain number of millions to his children, his wife didn't rate importantly. He freely admitted to intimates that he didn't care how or where he acquired wealth; he was out to get it by hook or crook. If such a life isn't a miserable failure in the eyes of both God and man, what is?"—B.C Forbes (1937).

There are two messages here. One, do whatever it is that you love to do, but also learn to play the game of life in the process. I have a great respect for Donald Trump and what he has accomplished, but I have even greater respect for a person like JAY Z and many others like him. The reason being is that Donald Trump was set up to succeed, due to the connections of his father. People like JAY Z were set up for failure, but they discovered the blueprint for success and that blueprint is doing what you love to do and there you will find happiness and wealth. I would like to offer you this thought taken from my book "How to Outsmart the Credit Bureaus."

I am a person who believes in the power of faith in God and yourself, because God is moved by faith not emotions. Albert Einstein once said, "Imagination is greater than knowledge because it is infinite." I disagree. I think that a person can dream and imagine a different circumstance his entire life, but without knowledge he will never find a way out of his situation. There are many people who do not know where they stand in life simply because they have no knowledge about themselves. They do not understand how powerful they can become. How a person is born depends on the favor of God. How a person dies depends on how he uses the favor that God has given him. You may be born a pawn, but you can die a queen. Where there is poverty, there is crime. Where there is crime, there is ignorance. Where there is ignorance, there are those seeking to exploit that ignorance? This keeps many at the finish line of life, even before they can begin to start the race and accomplish their dreams. Remember that chances are not always given to the most talented, smartest, strongest, or prettiest, but to those who learn to turn their own risk into chances to accomplish their dreams.

Made in the USA
San Bernardino, CA
03 December 2019